SLAVERY AND BLACK AMERICAN STATEHOOD

THE CREATION OF A BLACK AMERICAN HOMELAND IN LIBERIA

GEBAH SEKOU KAMARA

ARCHWAY
PUBLISHING

Archway Publishing books may be ordered through booksellers or by contacting:

Archway Publishing
1663 Liberty Drive
Bloomington, IN 47403
www.archwaypublishing.com
844-669-3957

Interior Image Credit: Alvin L. Sieh

ISBN: 978-1-4808-9251-4 (sc)
ISBN: 978-1-4808-9252-1 (e)

Library of Congress Control Number: 2020912705

Print information available on the last page.

Archway Publishing rev. date: 10/02/2020

CONTENTS

ACKNOWLDGEMENTS

I wish to thank Mr. Sanders, the FCI- Fairton camp librarian who saw my interest in studying the history of Liberia and the United States and he made sure to provide me with any reading materials that were related to African and Black American history. With his support and encouragement, I was able to make extensive use of the limited resources at the federal camp for my research. I also had the opportunity to have one-on-one conversations with many of the Black federal inmates residing at the facility who had tremendous insight into the social dynamic of America racial and political climate. These were individuals whom they and their forbearers had been impacted directly by racial and political policies of the American society.

I also want to thank my nephew, Ansumana Turay; my childhood friends and brothers, Momodu Gray, Victor Garflor and Lassana K. Dorley for their financial, spiritual and moral supports. I do not know what would had been my fate without them. Thanks also to Abdullah Konneh, my brother Karomo Kaba; my nephew Varney and his wife, Massa; also my sisters, Massa Konneh, Rukie Warity; my niece, Ajallatu Turay and her two wonderful daughters, Mariama and Josie; my son, Ishmail and his mother Mayboline, who, in their grace, were able to send me historical materials and books for the research for this book.

Many thanks to my friend Chidi Ezeobi, whose inspiration and courage were the main reasons that I was able to write this book during my adjustment in the federal prison work camp. He encouraged and challenged me to use my time wisely, assuring me that time flies and I would never have this much free time again, so he edged me to do something constructive. Chidi was not just talking the talk; he was a living example of how to engage your mind in a positive way when life knocks you down and the world turns its back on you. Chidi was locked up for nine years for trumped up charges that the U.S. government brought against him, but rather than steeping his mind in anger and hate, he put his time to positive use. He wrote over three books and thousands of poems and inspirational words during his period of incarceration.

I also want to thank my man, Mendeecees Harris, whose thirst for knowledge about Africa and the Black race powerfully convinced me to write this book. Many thanks to my Muslim brothers, Aladdin the Imam at Fairton, FCI, who kept me on my toes about performing my five daily prayers on time. Many thanks to Terence Thomas, whose vast knowledge about the history of Liberia was beyond that of any Black American person I have ever met. Thomas has a vast reservoir and great recollection of world history, especially Black history and the history that led to the creation of Liberia. I learned more about my birth country, Liberia, from Thomas than I did in all my schooling while in Liberia.

Finally, sincere thanks to all the friends and relatives who encouraged me to continue being engaged in writing and reading to avoid watching my time go by in slow motion. This book would never have been undertaken if not for the encouragement of my sons, Sekou, Ishmail, Kaden, and Zane, and my daughters Siyana and Tenneh Kamara. Nor could this project have been completed without the dedicated efforts of my best friend, Ngozi Atanmo, and my former bosses, Tracy and Dean, whose goodwill and kind words of support have kept me standing strong on my two feet.

THE SEAL OF THE REPUBLIC OF LIBERIA

The seal shows a sailing vessel approaching the coast, a palm tree, a plow and a spade on the shore; a dove on the wing with an open scroll in its claws, and the sun just emerging from the water. Above the emblem, the national motto reads: **The Love of Liberty Brought us Here,** and beneath it, the words, **Republic of Liberia**.

The symbols of the seal are obvious: a peace-bringing bird, the dove, arrives with a message from overseas (the United States of America), the granting of independence. The ship represents the arrival of the colonists, as does the national motto: The Love of Liberty Brought us Here. Also, the spade and the plough refer to the colonists, as they brought these tools with them. The palm tree may symbolize one of the main products of the region.

(*The Open-Door Policy of Liberia, an Economic History of Modern Liberia*; p.10, by Fred van der Kraai.)

THE LIBERIAN NATIONAL ANTHEM

Liberian National Anthem

Lyrics by Daniel Bashiel Warner (1815-1880)

All hail, Liberia, hail! (All hail!)
All hail, Liberia, hail! (All hail!)
This glorious land of liberty,
Shall long be ours.
Though new her name,
Green be her fame,
And mighty be her powers,
And mighty be her powers.
In joy and gladness,
With our hearts united,
We'll shout the freedom,
Of a race benighted.
Long live Liberia, happy land!
A home of glorious liberty,
By God's command!
A home of glorious liberty,
By God's command!

All hail, Liberia, hail! (All hail!)
All hail, Liberia, hail! (All hail!)
In union strong success is sure.
We cannot fail!
With God above,
Our rights to prove,
We will o'er all prevail,
We will o'er all prevail!
With heart and hand our country's cause defending,
We'll meet the foe with valour unpretending.
Long live Liberia, happy land!
A home of glorious liberty,
By God's command!
A home of glorious liberty,
By God's command!

INTRODUCTION

Liberia's contribution to the world and Black American has often been forgotten by the very people that it was established for. Many freed Blacks from the United States and beyond gave their lives for the founding of this beautiful coastal land in West Africa that is today known as the Republic of Liberia. But today's generation of Black Americans would rather visit or talk about Mexico and foreign lands than mention or admire their connection with Liberia. As a result, Africa's first modern democracy created by freed slaves from America has been left buried in long distant memories of past generations of heroes who laid their lives on the line to escape slavery, white prejudice and persecution. The research and the time needed by historians to digest the complex history of Liberia has not been fully appreciated by most of its younger generations on both side of the Atlantic Ocean.

Liberia should have the same significance to Black Americans as Israel's significance to European Jews and Jewish people who came from other parts of the globe to establish historical connections with the state of Israel. Some of the reasons that Liberia's old democracy is on life support is because it was long ago abandoned by the sons and daughters of the many freed people of color in other parts of the world who sailed away to what they thought were better opportunities. These freed people of color were running from racial prejudice and persecution in search of freedom and to establish a peaceful country of their liking. It was their love of liberty, freedom and equal rights that brought them to this costal land on the west coast of Africa.

Liberia should reclaim its rightful position in the world as one of the earlier contributors to modern democracy, and the declaration of freedom and liberty for all who set foot on her shores. Black Americans need to reconnect with Liberia, their ancestral homeland, to help keep its dying democracy alive. If Liberian democracy fails, it will not be because of lack of effort on the part of those who risked everything to create this small nation. Instead, it will be because of the old wound of the slavery mentality that is still buried and scarred in the minds of many offspring of Black Americans and indigenous Liberians as well.

I challenge every generation of Black Americans, Americo-Liberians and the indigenous Liberians to remember the jubilant voices of their forefathers when they gladly shouted,

"In joy and gladness, with our hearts united,
We will shout the freedom of a race benighted.
Long live Liberia, happy land!
A home of glorious liberty, by God's command!
A home of glorious liberty, By God's command!"

With these voices let us all be reminded to pick up the torches of freedom, liberty, and the pursuit of happiness for the entire Black race!

CHAPTER 1

Before the arrival of free Black slaves from America in 1822, Liberia was also known as the Grain Coast, and the Malagueta Coast, or the Pepper Coast. Much of Liberia's actual history has been forgotten or misrepresented from its inception.

Historians believe that before 1822 there were sixteen or more tribes living within the shoreline of what is today known as Liberia. The early people of the Grain Coast or Malagueta Coast were believed to have descended from the Pygmies, who were people of small size or height, according to the early traditions of many of the African tribes. Historical accounts that trace their existence on the western African coast are rare, and no recorded history exists that could prove their early existence in Liberia. However, tales and legends, along with numerous stories and memories of their existence, still live on in many West African villages and towns.

All around West Africa, stories and legends of these earlier inhabitants are carefully narrated and lamented amongst the various subcultures and tribes of the subregions. For example, in present-day Liberian stories and legends, they are referred to as *Jinna* or *Nee Gee*. In Senegal, they are called *Kondrong*, or *Komo Koudoumia* by the Wolof tribe. The Sousou in present-day Guinea refer to them as *Doki*.

Most early historical events were transmitted through oral expression or narratives of the elders. The legends and stories of the Pygmies still play an important educational role in the customs, religion, and traditions of most of the tribal cultures in Liberia and other West African countries. In many cultures in Liberia and the subregions, one cannot or tell a story without tying its origins back to the early inhabitants.

Historical records show that among the early tribes who arrived in Liberia were the Gola, who are believed to have traveled from the interior of Central

Africa. According to historical accounts, during the journey from the central regions of Africa to the western region, the Gola came across the Pygmies, who were bushmen dwelling in caves and the hollows of large trees. These early inhabitants lived mostly on fruits, the roots of wild trees, and animal flesh according to Abyomi Karnga, an historian of Liberia. Meanwhile, around 6000 BC, another group of people reportedly followed the Gola to the Grain Coast.

The origin of this second group is not noticeably clear. It is believed that they most likely came from the Sudan. The new migrants did not settle down well among the Gola and other tribes already settled on the coast. The new arrivals declared war on the Gola and other tribes, such as the Kissi. There are few historical details of the conflicts, after the defeat of the Gola, Kissi, and other tribes, the newly victorious group established an empire under the leadership of King Kumba, after whom the new settlers were named. The Kumba people thus comprised distinct groups, most of whom developed into different tribes after the death of King Kumba.

The cause of King Kumba's death is unclear, as is not uncommon when dealing with this period. But out of the breakaway groups came the Kpelle, the Lorma, the Gbande, Mende, and the Mano, all of whom belong to the same linguistic group. Contrary to some Western historians' accounts of the early inhabitants as lacking skills and existing in a primitive state, these groups were agriculturalist in their predominant skills. They were adept at using the land and fields to feed themselves without any so-called Western aids. In addition to their skills in agricultural production, they also developed arts such as pottery, weaving, and basket making. These early inhabitants of the Grain Coast were already using iron and metals before most peoples of Europe and the Americas. Their blacksmiths were far advanced in the production and crafting of spears, arrowheads, hoes, knives, rings, and iron rods.

Some Western historians refuse, perhaps out of ignorance, to highlight the imagination or skills of these early African inventors. With such remarkable craftsmanship, these early settlers achieved an advanced level of civilization. Bias causes some writers of West African history to assume that the early settlers of the coast or sub regions were primitive, without trade and commerce, unable to organize or rule each other, and lacking basic skills for human existence. Research has shown differently. Many anthropologists and historians have recanted these outdated beliefs and documented the existence of an advanced level of civilization among the earlier settlers of the Grain Coast or Malagueta Coast. Early Europeans in fact were taken aback by the level of commerce and the medium of exchange taking place on the West African coast. Historians mention that their blacksmiths were turning iron rods into shapes as a medium of exchange or money.

The adulterated claims of biased historians should not be taken at face value. An empire with trade and commerce and an intricate monetary system existed from an incredibly early period in Liberia. Civilization is a necessary way of life among a giving society. What is considered civilized in one part of the world may not be normal or acceptable within another society. Norms among Europeans, Chinese, or Arabs may not constitute an acceptable way of life among the Indians or the Africans, but the difference is not a dichotomy between "civilized" and "uncivilized."

Meanwhile, as migration continued, a third wave of people arrived and settled on the Pepper Coast, now Liberia. Among these groups were the Kru, Bassa, Dei, Mamba, and the Grebo tribes. According to historical accounts, this immigration to the coast originated in what is now the Ivory Coast. It is believed that mass immigration of tribes from Western Sudan arose after the medieval empires declined, following their conquest by the most powerful and well-equipped Moroccan armies, placing population pressure on smaller tribes, some of whom were engaged in tribal wars with each other.

Among the first tribes to arrive in this third group were the Kru. In the early sixteenth century, the Kru navigated by sea to the Grain Coast under extreme conditions. These early Africans, contrary to often misinformed European accounts, had the intellect and skills to navigate the rough Atlantic Ocean without requiring knowledge or technology borrowed from "white men" or Europeans, as has sometimes been thought.

A group or race demonized and labeled as primitive, unsophisticated, and uncivilized would not have been able to navigate a vast ocean without the help of any technology or navigational devices. How did they do it? How did they know where to locate Liberia? How did they develop the knowledge that their boats needed to withstand the beatings, torment, and velocity of the sea waves and conditions? Africans did not begin the course of human development after white colonizers stumbled upon them in caves. The contributions of Africa to the discovery of modern science and technology should not be hidden.

After the Kru arrived by sea in Liberia in the early sixteenth century, they were immediately followed by the Gredo, who also used the sea route. However, not all the members of the Gredo group traveled by sea, because some of the Gredo population were frightened by the dangerous waves of the Atlantic. Those who feared to travel on the ocean decided on a land route.

In the seventeenth century, the Mandinka were among the last tribes to begin arriving on the Grain Coast. Like the group they followed, the Mandinka were Muslims. Historians believe that the Mandinka people originated from the western Sudan region. They were a strong part of the Mali Empire before it fell to the Gao emperor Askia Mohammed in the sixteenth century. The Mandinka were among the few tribes with established written scripts in Black Africa. The Mandinka people were also advanced in arts, trade, education, and commerce.

CHAPTER 2

According to some early historians, the first contact the people of the subregion made with white European traders occurred as early as 520 BC, when Hanno the Carthaginian and his sailors landed on the West African coast. Historical accounts detail that the Carthaginian and his sailors may have sailed or landed near the coastal area of Cape Mount County, where he and his sailors encountered one of the tribes which at the time were believed to have settled in the area. The area of Cape Mount was first occupied by the Golas, who are believed to be the first inhabitants that traded with the Cartagena and his sailors.

Trade between the Cartagena's and the Golas is believed to be limited to just a few trade visits as documented by historians. Meanwhile, after Hanno the Cartagena reportedly made his first trade contact with the Golas, trade between the two races was not documented or reported until the 14th century, when trading between other European and the coastal tribes of Liberia became more frequent. Historical accounts also reveal that the Normans were the second group of foreigners who frequented the Liberian coastal areas and established temporary trading posts in the area. After building their trading posts on the Liberian coastal areas, the Normans began trading with the coastal tribes of the Grain Coast. The Normans bought ivory, gold, camwood, and peppers from the coastal tribes in exchange for salts and other commodities.

As Liberian coastal lands became more accessible to European traders, the Portuguese became the third foreign group to begin frequenting the Liberian coastal land. It is reported that the newly encountered Portuguese traders had significant influence over trades in the coastal area of the Grain Coast. For over a century the Portuguese had an absolute monopoly over the trade route before being replaced by much more dominant sea navigators such as the English, the French, and the Dutch. As the 15th century was in a waning phase, Portuguese,

Spanish, Dutch, English, and French traders and sailors became more frequent in the region. European traders and sailors interacted much more closely with the local inhabitants and they also accepted other traders from parts of the West African coastal areas. As the European traders' presence was felt among the people, so was their influence on the history of the region.

European traders and sailors had a considerable impact on the lives of the inhabitants of the coastal areas. Their impact was distinguishable and quite noticeable in the social and political arenas of the coastal regions. Not only did Portuguese traders have a monopoly over trading in the coastal regions, they also played a significant part in the partitioning and naming of some of the landmarks of the coastal area that are today important to the inhabitants of present-day Liberia. The Portuguese were involved in naming important landmarks, regions, rivers, and mountains, all of which to this day retain their original names. In present-day Liberia, the Portuguese named rivers such as the St. Paul, Montserrado, St. John, Cestor and the Cavalla. They also named the following places such as "Cabo Domonte," which is present-day Cape Mount, Cabo Montserrado for present-day Cape Montserrado, and Cabo das Palmas for present-day Cape Palmas.

Most of the coastal areas between Sierra Leone, Liberia and the Ivory Coast were often referred to by the names of their main commercial product. For example, Liberia was referred to as the "Malagueta Pepper," based on what was produced there at the time. The name was used interchangeably with the "Pepper Coast" or the "Malagueta Coast."

Meanwhile, the Dutch and the English preferred the name "Grains of Paradise Coast" as they frequented the areas. The Dutch and the English later came to name the region as the "Grain Coast." The Europeans assigned names to most of the coastal areas based on the commercial activities that were produced or taking place in the area. For example, the names of the coastal regions to the east of Cape Palmas were based on commercial products produced there. The Ivory Coast was so named because of its ivory products, and the "Gold Coast" because of its gold trade in Ghana. The Gold Coast later became called the Slave Coast when the slave trade was introduced to the region.

The European traders present in the region at the time exchanged textiles, beverages, alcoholic drinks, salts and general merchandise for the spices, gold, and ivory that were sought from coastal tribes. The medium of trade between coastal inhabitants and European traders was mainly done in battle trade; the coastal inhabitants' goods were exchanged for European goods, sometimes for an equal or lesser value. Since there was no established currency existing between the two races at the time, "Barter trade" became the preferred medium of exchange between the European and the coastal inhabitants.

Meanwhile, as the value and the demand of what was considered respectable trade and commerce degenerated, the barbaric and inhumane business of slave trading gave birth to a trade that would go on to hurt the African continent and deplete it of its human capital and resources. The new trade came to be viewed as highway robbery of African human resources by European criminal traders who the kind-hearted inhabitants of the coastal regions had come to consider as trading partners. As the mutual trading of products and goods came to an end, the ugly slavery trade soon came to replace the trading of goods and produce for human trafficking.

By the end of the 16th century, European maritime power frequenting the coastal region was willfully engaged in the most barbaric and inhumane commerce in all human history. In addition, this new commerce undertaken by European criminal traders on the African continent resulted in significant loss of intellect and talent of an estimated 20 million of its most productive sons and daughters that were led away in bondage to a place of no return.

The untold destruction resulting from the slave trade was more alarming than the mere loss of a vibrant number of its young and able-bodied population. The callous European slave trade drained the African continent by capturing, buying and the kidnapping by force of the young sons and daughters who were Africa's most productive and skilled workers, entrepreneurs, herbalists, blacksmiths, inventors, and midwives, among others. The illicit European slave trade left behind mostly old and feeble adults and children, who were defenseless against other slave traders that would later navigate the continent in search of free human labor. Young mothers were snatched away from nursing infants and placed in bondage to be brought into slavery in Europe and the Americas. Fathers and mothers were separated and lead to various slave-trading posts before being sold to other slave traders from Europe and the Americas.

As these vibrant sons and daughters of Africa were being stolen and violently kidnapped from their places of birth, their children were left with grandparents, relatives and the village residents, most of whom were old and feeble. These relatives and villagers were weak in many capacities and were left with no choice but the burden of raising a young generation of parentless children. As a result, many of these elderly adults did not live long enough to complete the task of raising those children, some of whom were forced to raise themselves. Those young people were ill-prepared and ill-equipped to resist the white oppressors and the systematic robbery of Africa's natural resources and minerals as they were extracted from their native soil to build Europe and the Americas.

Africa's young ill-prepared generation were also left unprepared to deal with the enormous issues that later emerged when slavery was abolished. For Africa, the damage was done; it was unprecedented and would take centuries to even begin solving the many problems that white oppression, slavery, and colonization brought upon the African continent. In many African societies and cultures, the elders, town chiefs or other villagers and community leaders often mediated disputes among the tribes, attempting to resolve emerging dispute amicably. But with the continent left with mostly inexperienced natives, hostilities between tribes brought about the disruption of the normal social order that had existed for centuries among them before the barbaric slave trade was introduced. Group hostilities among tribes ultimately resulted in famine, tribal wars and disrupted social coexistence among groups. Unfortunately, this epidemic of disrupted social order was a result of the slave trade and continues to hover over the current generation on the African continent.

Tribal differences, along with peoples' inability to defend themselves and settle disputes made the colonial rule easier to impose over most of African regions. Just like slavery itself, colonial rule was barbaric and inhumane. Imposition of the colonial system smothered the ability of the African people to self-govern. Colonialism, created impartial borders, imposed puppet governments and rulers who remotely controlled and manipulated native Africans to their liking. Some of these puppet leaders were cruelly insensitive to the plights of the people. Some subjugated their people by pitting tribes against each other while they and their white colonial masters surreptitiously continued to plunder the natural resources of their respective countries that was on going from the days of slavery.

The resulting breakdown and weaknesses among the natives arrogantly gave the colonizers reasons to justify to the rest of the world and to Africans themselves that their system of imperialism was best for Africa. White colonizers argued that Africans could not self-govern without European involvement. Although such an argument was blatantly false and demeaning to the Africans, some prejudiced writers of history have recorded these false claims in their writings and successfully sold those narratives to their audiences. At the same time, such false depictions and purposeful misrepresentations of Africa and the African people are not uncommon today in the history books of white colonizers.

Before the white slave traders and their colonizers ever set foot on African soil, the continent was being self-governed by chiefs, queens, and kings presiding over empires and kingdoms with a unique system of governing that met the needs of the people residing in its territories or regions. Before the white man's deliberate system of divide and conquer was introduced on the African continent, civilization and civil co-existence were the natural order of things before it was disrupted by the slave trade and the barbaric imposition of Western colonization on the continent.

Many historical and anthropological writings have documented the existence of a higher level of civilization in Africa before the arrival of the Europeans traders. As cited by Sir Harry Johnson: in his famous Explorer; West African Review, vol.29, and his report on Liberia (Vol 1) (1906), many historians have chronicled its history incorrectly. He mentions that historical documents leave no doubt that the people of the coastal region of Africa had accomplished an enviable and admirable standard of living and that people of the coastal areas made many products which were of higher quality than those produced in pre-industrial Western European countries during the same era.

According to the tradition of the Norman traders who visited Liberia in the fourteenth century, as well as in the authentic records of the Portuguese traders who came in early contact with the people of coastal Liberia, it was recorded that commerce before 1460 and 1560 reveals the existence of a high level of civilization and well-being amongst the untutored native's inhabitants.

This fact is contrary to what is found in many Western literature about present-day Africa, which still contrasts with the condition of the coastal areas in the early part of the nineteenth century, suggesting that the aggressive greed of the Europeans combined with the slave trade did much to brutalize and impoverish the coastal population during the two hundred years between 1670 and 1870. In Liberia, according to written records by Norman and Portuguese traders, inhabitants of the Liberian coastal lands were well-furnished with cattle, particularly in the northern area. They also had sheep, goats, and fowl, and are believed to have carried on a good deal of advanced agricultural practices. By looking at the agricultural skills of the early inhabitants of the coastal land, they could not have been complete savages as venally depicted by many ignorant Western historians of the past and present. Most of the historical accounts detailed at the time about the black continent show that Black people had no place in the curriculum of history.

Black people were presented by early Europeans historians as human beings of lower status, lacking intellect, and unable to show passion or a sense of reasoning. It was also portrayed that they were only useful to themselves and the white race when made to draw water and hew wood from the fields. For some of these ignorant writers of African history, no formal thought process was envisioned for the unique and multifaceted history of Africa and its people. Africa was a playground for exploitation and the clandestine extraction of its natural and human resources by Western powers.

To further their ugly narratives about Black Africa to the world, the Chicago World's Columbian Exposition of 1893 vividly displayed a false and ugly depiction of African history. Black Americans hoped that the exhibition would offer Blacks in America an opportunity to showcase to the world and white America their value and contribution to the world. However, they were left in a state of great disappointment by what the organizers of the expose decided to display about Africa and the Black race's contribution to the civilization of humanity. A display about "Uncivilized Dahomey Villagers" showcased inhabitants dressed in animal skins and half-naked as the highlight considered to define African contribution to the world. This purposeful display of barbaric ugliness of the Black race was a way for the racist white majority of America to depict the Black minority as people of a lower race and inferior in social status.

Unfortunately, growing up in Liberia there was limited availability of realistic portraits in literature or historical accounts of African accomplishments presented in a positive context. When mentioned at all, it typically occurred in the negative as a biased way of depicting a lower status of humanity. It is still difficult to source historical literature giving a truthful, unadulterated, impressive account of how Africans were the first to domesticate goats, sheep, and cows. Much of the lampoon literature gives a detailed description of accomplishments of the white race and virtually omits details about the accomplishments of Africans. When the teaching and discovery of science are discussed, Black Africans are often left out altogether. For example, the mentioned of how Africans assisted the Spanish and the Portuguese during their early exploration of the Americas is left out. But rather much praises are arrogantly attributed to Christopher Columbus as the greatest explorer of all time. The mention of one of the most celebrated black explorers of the

Americas Este 'ban, who traveled through the Southwest in the 1530s is often left out.

The beginning of scientific discovery and advancement from the various regions of the non-Black world are often mentioned in heroic narrative and with the arrogance of pride. Little is mentioned about the Black Africans' early development in the field of science. For example, little is mentioned about ancient Africans of the interior having sufficient knowledge about concocting poisons for arrowheads, extracting metals from nature and refining them for development in the industrial arts, and mixing durable colors for paints. Less is mentioned about the advancement of chemistry and methods the ancient Egyptians used to preserve their dead.

Some of the technologies of ancient Africans have been found by modern archaeologists and historians to be over thousands of years old and in good condition. Modern science from the West has not been able to replicate what the early Egyptians did with their dead in terms of their advanced methods of preservation. Not only did the Africans play a major role in the development of science, they also developed the idea of trial by jury, a practice of jurisprudence that is active in many modern democratic countries around the world to this day, including the United States. Black Africa also produced the first stringed instruments, and tools for navigation of the seas. Powerful kingdoms were developed, such as the Songhay empire, Timbuktu, Oyo, Ashanti, Dahomey, and the Congo with its rich culture, sophistication, and material wealth. These African cities were at one time major commercial and educational centers.

Significant commercial products from coastal regions in Africa as discovered by early Europeans sailors and traders have already been discussed. It is important to explore the types of goods that Europeans were able to offer to the Black African of the coastal regions.

From the fourteenth to the seventeenth centuries, when Europeans first stumbled upon the coastal regions, there were no cotton goods or calicoes in all their vessels. While this may sound strange to some readers, it was the African natives from the coastal area of present-day Gambia, Northern Guinea and present-day Cape Mount county in Liberia that impressed Europeans with their excellent cotton fabrics.

The Portuguese were so impressed that they took back with them cotton seeds from the coastal region of Africa. While no historical account survives to support this, it is possible that no cotton goods were exported from Europe to West Africa until the end of the seventeenth and beginning of the eighteenth centuries. Like most of Africa's natural resources and minerals, they are often extracted from African soil, brought to Europe and the Americas, and ultimately returned to the African continent only to be sold at exorbitant prices as finished goods or products. The cotton products described here were no exception.

Before European traders brought back finished cotton products to sell or exchange for other goods, natives of the subregions of Africa were very productive with their cotton industries. Weaving and dyeing of cotton products was faring well among native inhabitants of the coastal areas. However, when cotton goods from European countries such as Spain, Portugal, and Germany began to arrive on the continent, local cotton industries of weaving and dyeing suffered from the influx of foreign cotton products.

As demand for African cotton and other trade goods was slowing down as early as the time of Ca' da Mosto (middle of the fifteenth century), white traders began carrying heavy cannons on their vessels and would often fire them as they approached the coastal trading posts around the subregion areas. The loud and strange sound of the cannon would frighten the natives. This was a bellicose tactic of intimidation designed to drive down the cost of goods and make the natives succumb to quick deals and lower prices.

The early Europeans were not only responsible for the naming of places, the exchange of products, the introduction of firearms and the barbaric kidnapping and forceful capture of millions of Africa's sons and daughters to strange lands, they were also responsible for the introduction and spreading of many unknown diseases on the continent. These afflictions included dysentery, syphilis and certain other parasites unknown to the Black race. In addition, introduction of the slave trade led to hostilities and the empowerment of some dominant tribes who were susceptible to influence over other tribes. It is sad to note that the remnants of the hostilities created as the result of European manipulation and slaveholders' profit-making ventures somehow contributed to tribal divisions still experienced today in Liberia and many other parts of Africa.

In the case of Liberia, the Golas, Kru, Kpelles and the Kissi tribes were notorious slave traders. They were known for conspiring with unscrupulous Europeans who, in their desperation for free slave labor and profits, looted the coastal areas of West Africa for their victims. The slave traders and their unscrupulous native allies did not tangle with all the tribes, especially the native tribes of the northern coastal areas. Because of the history of cannibalism that some tribes were known for, slave hunters and their allies were frightened to venture into their territories.

However, in the mix of those abstruse environments, free and newly emancipated slaves from the United States of America arrived on an American ship under the guidance of the American Colonization Society (ACS) in 1820. The newly freed men and women came from America where their Black African ancestors were sold into slavery. The arrival of the first colonists of free Blacks on Liberian soil began the start of a Black-owned modern democracy on the African continent.

CHAPTER 3

WHY THE WHITEMAN CAME LOOKING FOR SLAVES IN AFRICA

The first white settlers in the Virginia colony of Jamestown in 1619 were desperate for free laborers to cultivate their land to grow food for basic survival. The historical account details that in the winter of 1609 to 1610, the weather was extremely difficult. As the threat of starvation loomed over them, the settlers roamed the area hunting for wild berries, nuts and elevated graves to eat the corpses of their dead. Most of the settlers succumbed as food became increasingly unavailable. Nearly five hundred settlers were reduced in number to scarcely sixty according to a report from the House of Burgesses of Virginia in its 1619 document, which provided detailed accounts of the first twelve years of the Jamestown colony. A settlement of about one hundred inhabitants was served only a small handful of barley per meal.

The food situation in the colony became scarcer still when more people from England arrived in the small colony. Many of the new arrivals in the Virginia colony lived in cave-like holes dug into the ground. Historical accounts of their living conditions in the winter of 1609 to 1610 revealed that they were driven by extreme hunger that caused them to subsist on things that were unimaginable to most humans. In his famous book title (A People's History of the United States by Zinn, Howard,1(922-2010), accounts detail that some of the starving settlers ate human flesh and excrement for survival. Some ate other humans whose hunger had enfeebled them with no chance of survival. Settlers dug up the graves of others who had recently starved to death in search of food. Consumed by the hand of hunger, one of the settlers is said to have slain his wife as she slept. He cut her into pieces and salted her body, eating every portion of her flesh, leaving only her head untouched according to the historian Zinn Howard.

Thirty of the colonists submitted a petition to the House of Burgesses by objecting to the twelve-year governorship of Sir Thomas Smith. The Burgesses replied, "In those 12 years of Sir Thomas Smith, his government we aver that the colony, for the most part, remained in great want and misery under most severe and cruel laws . . ."

Allowances for the settlers during that period were mostly small amounts food, which consisted of about eight ounces of meal and a half pint of peas per day. Much of the food that was distributed was rotten and infected with maggots. Due to the hardships they bore, some settlers wandered into native Indian territory, despite fear that the natives were brutal. Some of those who ventured out in this way were killed or beaten and tied to trees until they died of starvation. In such a stark environment, the Virginia settlers needed free laborers to plant corn and tobacco crops for subsistence and trade, especially as their population was dwindling as more people fled to escape prosecution in England.

At the time, the settlers were just discovering the skills to grow and harvest tobacco on their land. By 1617, they completed their first harvest of tobacco and dispatched the first cargo shipment to the mainland of England. To their great satisfaction, their harvest generated a substantial amount of profit to improve their barren existence and continue the lucrative crop generation. Based on the first profit margin, they were hoping to expand their efforts to the growth of other crops. They knew that their path to success and profit depended on the availability of manpower, which was an obstacle for the new colony at that time. To expand the profit yield from their crops they needed more manpower. Ideally, they needed free labor—something the small settlement could not provide.

During that developmental period, there was an insufficient number of white servants in the colony to serve as free laborers. The settlers did not have the ability to influence or coerce the Indians to work on their fields. Even though the white settlers were superior in weaponry, they were outnumbered by the native American Indian population at the time. They also knew that conflict with the Indians would cause many casualties to themselves, and they could not afford any further reduction in population.

Another advantage that the native Indians had over the increasingly desperate white settlers was the resiliency and ability to skillfully cultivate their land. They had long known the skills to seed and propagate their land far better than the white settlers, whose experience and knowledge of the new land were far less. Despite the desperation for additional labor to grow their crops, they accepted that it would be difficult, if not impossible, for them to capture and enslave the native American Indians. In the colony, there were few white indentured servants who had contracted for the right to passage to America. These servants were free to start a new life in the colony once their contract was served (typically four to seven years).

The white settlers were confronted with a difficult situation; they needed a solution to continue growing their crops not only to sell, but to feed themselves. As they grew frustrated by their inability to support themselves, they began enacting laws to force the free settlers work for them. Most of those free settlers were skilled craftsmen who knew little about cultivating the land for crop growth, unlike the native Indians. The Indians' ability and superiority in cultivating the land and sustaining their population caused resentment against the desperate white English settlers. According to Edmund Morgan, in his book, *American Slavery, American Freedom,* "If you were a colonist, you knew that your technology was superior to the Indians; you knew that you were civilized, and they were savages, but your superior technology had proved insufficient to extract anything from your deprived conditions."

By 1619, nearly one million black Africans were already enslaved on plantations in South America. The Portuguese were among the first Europeans to encounter Africans living along the coastal land of the West African subregion. During their exploration of Africa coastal regions, they brought back to Lisbon with them ten black Africans as slaves. That event, as later accounted by historians, started the African slave trade industry in Europe and the Americas.

The Africans captured as slaves were mostly terrified, hopeless and helpless in their new environment, which made their enslavement easier for men who claimed to be their owners. Sadly, many of these Africans were violently removed from their land, families, customs, cultures, and religions. All the things that make a complete person were extracted and disregarded. The desperate sons and daughters of Africa were plucked from the only life that they had known and forced into a world where the language, climate, dress, culture, and people were far different than anything they had ever known.

Despite unimaginable conditions, many managed to survive. Prejudiced white writers of Black history would have you believe that the black Africans brought as slaves were uncivilized savages and that by the grace of almighty white power, slavery was introduced and suddenly Blacks began to learn and embrace civilization. This is the distorted picture that some writers of Black history want you to believe. Unfortunately, they mastered these falsehoods for centuries through their powerful media propaganda. Some members of the Black race swallowed these falsehoods and accepted them at face value.

Throughout the period of slavery in America, many white politicians, historians and ordinary whites continued to harbor these false beliefs about the Africans brought here as slaves. Some still maintain that belief system even today. The truth is that before white settlers set foot on the land that is now America, the native American Indians were the original inhabitants of the land. White English settlers were not brought here in bondage and stripped of their identities. Most of them came here voluntarily, bringing along with them their culture, customs, religion, and way of life. And for those whites who were later brought to America as servants, they were already familiar with the culture that they were settling into, because they were of the same cultural and ethnic heritage. Those servants, however, later earned their right to freedom after their contracts as servants ended. Most of the servants who were newly freed could settle in the new world as freedmen and women, earning the right and power to determine their destinations and future.

Black Americans, on the other hand, were not afforded the luxuries of being free and having a voice in their own affairs. Unlike white servants who mostly came voluntarily, African Americans were brought into America as cargo. They were sick, beaten, humiliated, starved, terrified, and their way of life was forcefully stamped out. What some of the ill-informed writers of Black history failed to mention is that any human being terrorized, tortured, beaten and violently removed from their heritage under the threat of violence, and forced to travel the rough seas under extreme weather conditions, would undoubtedly undergo psychological or physical erosion of some kind. The fact that Black American slaves endured more than two hundred years of hardship and suffering under systematic enslavement speaks to the relentless spirit and fortitude of the Black race's intelligence and unflinching will to survive.

Most of the slave hunters and traders were men of abject ignorance about their own cultures, politics and social life. With such limited awareness of their own culture, one can understand why they were willfully ignorant of the strange pristine and organized social and political life of the West African people. It has been historically documented that when most of Africa was living under civilization and social order, most Europeans were still living in caves and engaged in primitive life. None of the African or enslaved Africans ever referred to themselves as ignorant or savages, but it was the unenlightened slave hunters and traders who referred to them as such.

Despite the slave hunters' endless determination through their superior military means, they were unable to venture into most of the interior portions of the African coast. They succeeded mostly by conspiring to trade with some of the notorious chefs and tribes, who, for nefarious reasons were known to be prolific slave traders themselves. Like most ancient civilizations of the past, Africa had an advanced civilization and culture that was comparable to that of Europe, the Mediterranean, and Persia. Because of Africa's intricate culture and customs, its society was greatly admired by those Europeans who came seeking trade on the coast. Despite its advanced cultures and civilizations, cruelties and the privileged class system had its grip on the religion, politics and social life of the people. During those antebellum years, ancient Africa was a civilization of nearly 100 hundred million inhabitants. The Africans' use of iron and their admirable skills in agriculture, weaving, dyeing, ceramics, sculpture, and arts were enough to duly impress the European traders.

In the 16th century when most of Europe was still struggling and only starting to leapfrog into modern nations and states, the African kingdoms of Mali, Timbuktu and the Songhay were already stable with organized trade routes, religious and educational centers known to the world. The kingdoms had their own large urban and trading centers that were often flooded by merchants from the Middle East and India trading and exchanging knowledge with each other. The acknowledgment of Africa's advanced culture and civilization was known by the authorities and the inhabitants of Nice, France. This was proved when the secretary to the rulers wrote transcripts to merchants in Italia in 1563 urging them to do business with the kings of Mali and Timbuktu.

Mali and Timbuktu assured the Italian merchants that they and their goods and ships would be treated well and granted the favors that their leaders requested. This was a clear indication that the African leaders were good and fair businesspeople before the Europeans introduced corruption and unfair business practices that only benefited themselves to the detriment of the African continent and people. Italian rulers were aware of the culture and advanced civilizations of the people of Mali and Timbuktu. They knew that the people on the African continent were not savages and ignorant. According to a Dutch report which is believed to have been written around 1602, the country of Benin was described in the coastal area of Africa as follows: "In Benin, which was one of the advanced kingdoms within the West African Coast, the town seemed to be very great when you enter it. You go into a great broad street, not paved, which seemed to be seven or eight times broader than the various streets in Amsterdam.

"The houses in this town stand in order, one close and even with the others, as the houses in Holland stand; very civil and good-natured people, easy to be dealt with, condescending to what Europeans will civilly require of them, and very ready to return double the presents we make them." These were the words that some Europeans travelers used to describe the people on the coastal land of Guinea in 1680.

It might be surprising for some readers that are unfamiliar with the culture of the West African coastal people that the current inhabitants of Guinea and the surrounding countries of the coastal areas to this date exhibited to a great extent those same characteristics of their ancestors. The Africans celebrated communal relationships, building strong family ties based on love, desire, and commitment to help one another, greatly emphasizing a culture of *our, us and we,* rather than me and me, or an individualistic mindset. In the African communal society fishing, weeding, harvesting, canoeing, playing or games, or pounding of grains are done as group activities and out of a desire to harness the feeling of togetherness.

The values of generosity and forgiveness were the order of the day and greatly encouraged by the people. The idea of prison and the death penalty was foreign to the African of that time, but it was imported by European colonizers as a way of instilling fear and control over the people they ruthlessly ruled over. The holding of hatred or malice was abhorred by the community. There were always arms open wide to welcome strangers and travelers, and they would go beyond extraordinary steps to provide for them what was at their disposal. It was through this virtue of generosity and good spiritedness that the European traders and slave hunters took advantage of them. Tradition and custom were powerful institutions that were respected by every member of the community. Each member had a unique part to play in keeping the institutional rituals of the tribal life and customs alive. In the ancient African society, disharmony within was understood to bring harmful consequences from the kings, tribal leaders, Zoes and the spirit world of the ancestors. Issues involving the entire tribal community were the responsibility of the clan or village and were resolved by kings, spiritual leaders, and clan elders. The tribal community meted out public punishment for transgression of tribal norms and customs. As described, one can arguably agree that Africans could resolve their own conflicts. It is perplexing to see African countries and leaders seeking the aid of their formal European colonizers and the United States or the so-called United Nation or some Harvard University graduated personality to resolve current and past conflicts. Often these individuals and countries take side, fuel the conflict with their westernized conflict resolution experiments and become impartial negotiators. For some of these countries their economy depends on the continuation of wars, conflict and poverty on the African continent. Wars and poverty on the African continent help amass wealth for western gun and food manufactures.

Meanwhile, unlike the European continent of the same period, which had just arrived out of the Greek and slave societies which quickly tore down and rendered useless its tribal and communal societies and cultures; the African continent was different. As for Africa, it still had its tribal customs and communal style of life in order. The issues of laws, justice, and punishments were administered with a sense of kind-heartedness and compassion to apply sanctions to deter would-be offenders. According to Basil Davidson who wrote the book *The African Slave Trade*, he described punishment in Europe in the early part of the sixteen centuries as being brutal when compared to the Congo-Africa in the same period. Davidson described that in Portugal and England where personal property ownership was taking the forefront, a small child could be hanged for stealing a rag of cotton. So, the idea of compassion in the administration of justice was something introduced and exemplified by the Africans, not earlier Europeans according to Davidson.

CHAPTER 4

WHITE SLAVE HUNTERS ON THE AFRICAN COAST

As European and American plantation owners became desperate for free labor to amass greater profit and control, it became apparent to slave hunters and traders that to be successful, they would have to venture into the African coastal lands. First in this venture were the Portuguese, Dutch and English. These three slave-trading peoples dominated the slave-trading industry during that era. The English were sailing more than a hundred ships on the coast of Africa by 1795. It is believed that the English accounted for half of the European slave trade from the African continent. The slave commerce in Liverpool, England was the most successful profitable venture for the English people at that period. The price of slaves on the coast varied but was mostly exorbitant due to the feeding of the crew on the middle passage, which came to ten shillings per head, and the cost of freight was £3.5 shillings.

The profit generated by the sale of each slave in the English colonies generated well over 30 percent—far more profit than any known existing business at that same time. Between 1783 and 1793 the overall profit generated from the sale of slaves in the English town of Liverpool amounted to 303,737 slaves sold, or nearly three million British pounds, or about three hundred thousand pounds per annually. This tremendous return of wealth to the English of Liverpool was the price that Black Africans paid in the flesh and blood of its sons and daughters to give England a head start in wealth creation and conquest to maintain its position as one of the superpowers of in the world.

The overall income from slave trade in 1790 was estimated to be seven-and-a-half million pounds for Liverpool alone. As abolition grew imminent, the merchant slave traders shipped forty-nine thousand, two hundred thirteen slaves (49,213) from Africa to the Sugar Islands using one hundred eighty-five vessels for their transport. Great Britain officially abolished slavery in May of 1807, which finally put an end to the ugly, barbaric practice of selling African men and women as commodities. Meanwhile, as the British were winding down their involvement in slave-trading, America was just entering into what was at that time a very lucrative business for plantation owners and politicians in the United States. In 1837, the first American slave ship, called the *Desire,* sailed to coastal Africa in search of slave cargo.

The *Desire* was described as split into racks, two feet by six feet, with leg irons, and bars. As American plantation owners and slave merchants eagerly joined their European counterparts in the infamous slave trade, by the 1800s nearly 15 million Black Africans had been transported as slaves to the Americas. As the slave trade became a major commerce of the emerging western powers, nearly 50 million sons and daughters of Africa were lost to death and disease as a result of slavery. Ironically, this period is described by historians as the start of modern western civilization.

As slave merchants arrived at their trading posts, African men and women were marched to the coastal areas, some walking subdued and frail for miles, while others were dragged to board the slave ships or vessels waiting to take them into slavery. Under the threat of the slave hunters' guns and whips, they were shackled around the neck and left standing in ill-fitting cells while the ocean wind, heat and salt spray relentlessly chafed their skin while they stared at each other, terrified, awaiting arrival at a place of no return. All these kidnapped and captured African sons and daughters were kept in cages until they were sold to slave traders from America and Europe.

A perfect description of the cages that were used on the Gold Coast to hold Africans before they were sold was detailed by a Frenchman named John or Jean Barbot's Description of the Coasts of North and South Guinea, published in 1732. "As the slaves come down from the inland countries, they are put into a booth or prison—near the beach, and when the Europeans are to receive them, they are brought out into a large place, where the ship's surgeons examined every part of each of them, down to the smallest members, men and women being stark naked. Such as allowed good and sound are set on one side and marked on the breast with a red-hot iron, imprinting the mark of the French, English, Dutch, Portuguese or American companies. The branded slaves are returned to their former booths where they await shipment, sometimes waiting for ten to fifteen days before shipment."

Meanwhile, the captured and sold Africans were picked, branded and readied for shipment like cattle. They were placed aboard and arranged in tiny spaces in the cargo areas of the awaiting ships. Some of these spaces they were placed in on the ships were described as just slightly larger than a human coffin. Chained together in tight spaces, most of them choked in the stench of their own waste.

Some historical documents gave more horrific accounts of their conditions as follows; in the publication " Aboard a Slave Ship, 1829 Eyewitness to History" one Reverend Walsh's account as he boards the slave ship: "The first object that struck us was an enormous gun, turning on a swivel, on deck- the constant appendage of a pirate; and the next were large kettles for cooking, on the bows- the usual apparatus of a slaves. Our boat was now hoisted out, and I went on board with the officers. When we mounted her decks, we found her full of slaves. Our boat was now hoisted out, and I went on board with the officers. When we mounted her, we found her full of slaves. She was called the Feloz, commanded by captain Jose' Barbosa, bound to Bahia. She had taken in, on the coast of Africa, 336 males and 226 females, making in all 562 and had been out seventeen days, during which she had thrown overboard 55. The slaves were all enclosed under grated hatchways between decks. The space was so low that they sat between each other's legs and were stowed so closed together that there was no possibility of their lying down or at all changing their position by night or day.

As they belonged to and were shipped on account of different individuals, they were all branded like sheep with the owner's marks of different forms. These were impressed under their breasts or on their arms, and, as the mate informed me with perfect indifference 'burnt with the red-hot iron. 'Over the hatchway stood a ferocious- looking fellow with a scourge of many twisted thongs in his hand, who was the slave driver of the ship, and whenever he heard the slightest noise below, he shook it over them and seemed eager to exercise it. Walsh when on to say, I was quite pleased to take this hateful badge out of his hand, and I have kept it ever since as a horrid memorial of reality, should I ever be disposed to forget the scene I witnessed. As soon as the poor creatures saw us looking down at them, their dark and melancholy visages brightened up. They perceived some-thing of sympathy and kindness in our looks which they had not been accustomed to, and feeling instinctively that we were friends, they immediately began to shout and clap their hands. One or two had picked up a few Portuguese words, and cried out, "viva! Viva!" The women were particularly excited. They all held up their arms, and when we bent down and shook hands with them, they could not contain their delight; they endeavored to scramble up on their knees, stretching up to kiss our hands, and we understood that they knew we were come to liberate them.

Some, however, hung down their heads in apparently hopeless dejection; some were greatly emaciated, and some, particularly children, seemed dying. Walsh described the circumstance which struck us most forcibly was how it was possible for such a number of human beings to exist, packed up and wedged together as tight as they could cram".

Others described the slave ships lengths as eighteen inches between decks, so that the unfortunate human beings couldn't turn around, or even onto their side, the elevation being less than the breadth of their shoulders; and here they are usually chained to the decks by the necks, legs, and tums. In such an environment the sense of misery and suffocation is so great that the African slaves are driven to frenzy, the voyage to their enslavement into America was covered with endless pain and suffering." Many were weak and infirmed due to their inhumane treatment. These were the accounts of numerous historians about the condition of the departing Africans.

Many of the African slaves who, by God's mercy, managed to survive the serious life and death diseases on board, ended their suffering by suicide or by jumping overboard into the dark ocean. Many would arrive at the respective places of their disembarking suffering from the bloody flux, a violent form of dysentery that caused blood to pour out of the anus. A case is documented of a slave captain, skilled in deception, who would plug the anuses of violently sick slaves with cotton wool so that they would be passed and appear untainted for possible buyers. Some of the sailors described the sea journey as seeing slaves in various positions of suffocation. In their desperate attempts at gasping for breath, chained together at the neck and feet, they suffocated each other to the death as they frantically sought for life's most important substance, *air*. In their desperate attempts to breathe air, many of the African slaves jumped overboard into the vast ocean to drown themselves as a blessed way out of their agonized existence.

Some sailors detailed witnessing the African slaves held in their tight spaces on board the decks of the ships covered with bloody excrement and mucus and reported that it resembled "a meat slaughterhouse." These horrific conditions and detailed accounts from the sailors did not discourage the white plantation owners in America about the inhumanity of the commerce of trading slaves that they were heavily engaged in. In their abject failure to enslave the Native American Indians, the forced kidnapping and violent immigration of African sons and daughters as slaves offered a more suitable and greater profit potential for American plantation owners and their scheming racist political supporters.

CHAPTER 5

WHY BLACK AMERICANS RETURNED TO AFRICA, WHERE THEY HAD NEVER BEEN

Photo by: Alvin L. Sich

A detailed account of the carnage in Santo Domingo states that it lasted for nearly two weeks. Meanwhile, destruction on both sides did not bring that rebellion to an end. In retaliation, white slave owners and French soldiers stationed on the island and nearby plantations began massacring and capturing slaves participating in the revolt. As news of the revolt spread like wildfire to other plantations, many more slaves joined the rebellion against their oppressors. As the revolt escalated into surrounding towns and plantations over two months, the slaves accelerated their attacks by slaughtering thousands more Caucasians, moving on to violently destroy nearly 200,000 acres of sugar cane, coffee and indigo plantations owned by slave masters. (U.S. Dept. of States Bureau of Public Affairs 2018).

The Haitian slave rebellion of 1791 was an epic turning point leading to the Haitian revolution that followed. In the wake of the carnage and bloodshed, African slaves were able to control nearly a third of the island. The French legislative assembly, many of whose members were newly elected, sensed the loss of their brutal grip on the enslaved population, which would certainly threaten their economic power and interests. This body quickly moved to grant civic and political rights to the "Freemen of Color" within their colonies. In the intervening period, news of the Haitian slave rebellion sent a chill down the spines of all slave owners in the western hemisphere, including the United States of America. Politicians and other leaders were all concerned about their Black slave populations.

Slave revolts on American plantations were not as frequent and if they did occur, it was never as large and extreme as those in the French and British controlled islands. However, when news of the African slave uprisings was disseminated in Europe and America, fear and confusion sent a shock wave among plantation owners, politicians, and most of the white population. For Americans, they were most afraid of being invaded by Toussaint, who is described as a bloodthirsty African brute who waged war on the strong French and British soldiers. Plantation commerce based on tobacco growing that originally started in the early Virginia colony had expanded into the popular, profitable cotton industry in most southern states. More southern states depended on cotton commodities for wealth and power than on tobacco.

The United States government depended heavily on taxed proceeds from cotton and tobacco prior to the industrial revolution. It is depressing to say that these new industries also depended on the free labor of African sons and daughters, that were forcibly removed from their native land and sold into slavery. The American white majority population and southern plantation owners feared the possibility of their slaves joining or concocting a Francois Dominique Toussaint type rebellion in America. To deal with any potential uprising from the enslaved Blacks, most southern states, including northern state slave owners, devised ingenious and harsh punishment for their enslaved Black property.

Laws were passed to control slaves from gathering, including restricting their movements. In those days, slaves already had control of slave movement, and they mostly stayed together. It was threatening to the white majority population to see a group of Blacks gathering.

Ironically after 300 hundred years in today's modern America, many white

Americans are still afraid to see groups of Blacks gathered without fearing for their safety. Meanwhile, new stringent restrictions on American Blacks and enslaved populations still did not stop them from sneaking together in groups whenever the opportunity presented itself. In some states, restrictions on the slaves' movements did not stop what is believed to be one of the largest slave revolts in the United States.

In January of 1811 during a ferocious downpour on a cold, windy late Tuesday evening, about four to five hundred Black slaves gathered near New Orleans after staging a rebellion at the plantation of Major Manuel Andry. At the time he owned more than eighty black slaves, more than any other slaveholder in St John the Baptist Parish. The slaves, armed with axes, knives, canes, and clubs attacked the plantation owner Andry and killed his son. As their numbers grew, they forcibly marched from plantation to plantation attacking the overseers. But the slaves' march came to an end when the United States military and local militia forces that were aware of the Toussaint revolts in Haiti, moved in and attacked and killed sixty-six of the slave rebels on the spot. In a mixed frenzy, slaves ran for their lives to nearby bushes. Sixteen of them were apprehended and shot to death by firing squad.

In 1822, Black slaves were implicated in another conspiracy to escape from enslavement. A freed slave named Denmark Vesey was believed to have conspired with other free Blacks as well as enslaved Blacks to burn down what was then considered America's sixth largest city at the time. The alleged plan was to initiate a major slave revolt in the city of Charleston, South Carolina. According to a one account, thousands of Black slaves were conspirators in the alleged plot. However, the plan was eventually aborted before Blacks began to assemble for the revolt. According to historian Herbert Aptheker, thirty-five Black slaves, including the alleged mastermind Denmark Vesey, were apprehended and sentenced to death by hanging.

As fear of slave uprisings continued to echo through southern plantations and cities, including northern cities, the concern remained that if slave uprisings continued, plantation slaves and free Blacks would become emboldened and resist their current barbaric status in America. It must be mentioned, though, that in the mix of threats of slave uprisings, no major revolts against the majority white population on the same level of the Haitian revolution occurred. News of Black slave uprisings became a defining motivation for the white population and plantation owners to treat the American minority Black population with hatefulness and violence, using potential uprisings as justification for their actions against them.

The southerners' mistreatment of Blacks also exacerbated their fears of an uprising that could be unleashed if many Blacks were allowed free. The thought of freed slaves dominated Southerners' fears that freed Blacks would encourage their former counterparts into an insurgency against white slaveholders. As abolitionist ideas began to creep into the southern consciousness, fear that the imposition of abolitionist ideas could spell disaster for the profitable enslavement business. For that reason, slaveholders resented northern abolitionists for economic reasons as well as for the protection of their own southern pride and traditions.

With slavery more vital for the economics and pride of the American south than the north, abolitionist ideas were unwelcomed anywhere in slaveholding states. Abolitionist advocates, sympathizers, or free Blacks caught tampering with the enlightenment of enslaved Blacks, or found randomly roaming through southern cities and towns, were immediately attacked with abrupt violence at the hands of white mobs.

The American south was deeply entrenched in the accumulation of wealth through the free labor of enslaved Blacks, and it was determined not to forgo its practices if they could at all help it. And for those Northerners or abolitionists who were determined to disrupt the Southerners' slave commerce, "lynching" and other forms of violent punishment awaited the disruptors. Sympathizers of abolitionist ideas caught in southern towns were also lynched. It is noteworthy to mention that the fear of a Black uprising was not just a concern of southern states alone. Some northern states also had apprehensions about Black slave revolts. Those states engaged in slavery also feared that their slaves would follow the example of the French colonies' slave revolts and grow in spirit to stage their rebellions against the white population enslaving them.

In a frenzy, in 1712 New York City acted in response to a failed insurrection planned by its enslaved Blacks. However, the insurrection was never carried out before being thwarted by the white population.

As a result of the failed revolt, New York City carried out a drastic punishment by hanging thirteen Blacks, burning three more Black men at the stake, and starving another Black man to death. So, frightened by the draconian punishment of their coconspirators, six of the suspected insurgents opted to commit suicide as one way out of their torment.

During this unsettling Antebellum period in the history of America, the protective barriers for social intolerance were on the rise. Violence against Blacks was on the increase in nearly every corner of American society. Northern cities in the United States became epicenters for race riots. Polling places were often the center for many labor disorders, fist fighting and the white man's demonstrations against the presence of Blacks.

Many whites were easily irritated and annoyed by the presence of freed Black slaves in their communities, some of whom were heavily engaged in exercising their rights and demanding their freedom and right to vote for the first time as free Americans. Many of the white population's premeditated social disorder and violence against free and enslaved Blacks did not meet the satisfaction of white Americans until "mob lynching" took center stage as a preferred form of punishment. Mob lynching was also effectively violent against other whites who were suspected of assisting slaves or harboring emancipation views for enslaved Blacks.

As racial tension brewed in the United States, an angered lynch mob went after Elijah P. Lovejoy, who was an abolitionist and vociferous in the cause for Black freedom. An angered white mob killed Lovejoy when he was identified as an abolitionist. Lovejoy's death stung the nation's sensibilities about the rise of mob lynching.

Furthermore, mob lynching was tolerated as an acceptable form of punishment against Blacks not only in southern states but in northern states as well. One recorded mob lynching of a freed Black man occurred in Massachusetts, a northern state that was considered the main transport route for slavery into America. According to observer accounts of a mob lynching which occurred in 1741, a Black man was accused of stealing some money. He was tied to a tree and beaten severely in order to extricate a confession from him. He was later brought down from the tree and later died of his wounds on his slave master's property.

During those heated periods in the American race conflict, many permanent Black and white abolitionists came close to being lynched by angry white lynch mobs, who were on the rampage meting out their form of white justice on free Blacks and enslaved Blacks accused of anything as mundane as looking at a white woman or for not saying, "Yes, sir," to a white man.

Frederick Douglass narrowly escaped execution by angered white lynch mobs when he and other free and enslaved Blacks were caught attempting to escape on the Eastern Shore of Maryland. The ingenious plan of Douglass's master helped save his young life from being taken by the angered mob.

Frederick's master skillfully diverted the attention of white members of the committee investigating whether the attempted escape was an insurrection.

White mobs also had other ingenious and cruel forms of punishment available for use against their Black victims. A court in Georgia sentenced a Black man to castration and deportation in 1827 (Macon Daily Telegraph). Other forms of barbaric punishment carried out by whites against Blacks in the state of Missouri entailed the cutting off ears, eye-gouging, and branding of the victim—all part of the modus-operandi of people in some southern states. In those states Blacks were killed or lynched for reasons such as accusing a white man of sleeping with a person's relative, daughter or wife even with clear proof. Almost any offense—even imagined—was enough to punish an enslaved or free Black person.

For example, a Black who accused a white person of fathering a child or children with his wife or other Black females could be lynched, even though the evidence might be apparent by the mixed-race appearance of the child in question. Many southern and northern white males and females had taste or sexual desire for a Black person, male or female. Many incidences of white men and white women forcing themselves onto their enslaved or domestic workers were quite common.

Race breeding by whites was evident by the offspring of many poor Black women. Their families were forced to raise the mixed child and sometimes the women or their family were chastised when it became apparent that the child was the offspring of a race breeding. The cyclical nature was that it was acceptable for white men to find pleasure in their desire for Black servants or slaves; however, it was undesirable for Black men to have any sexual desire for a white person. A Black accused of sleeping or making a gesture at a white woman was sufficient evidence for that person to be lynched by white mobs, who in their sick and corrupted minds were defending the virtue of the white woman and the white race.

A Black slave man named Joiners wrote a letter to his master's wife and daughter when he realized that "Union Army forces were approaching their cities and towns." In his letter, Joiner promised to take the daughter and mother to a "safe place" to protect them from the Union force's rapid advance. The daughter was 18 years old at the time and single. The amazing thing about Joiner is that he had taught himself how to write, which was a forbidden crime for Black people in many states at the time, including South Carolina, where Joiner's story was reported to have occurred. It was forbidden to teach a Black slave or person how to read or write. Joiner's letter was, however, intercepted and he was tried for making a pass at his master's wife and daughter.

Joiner was, however, exonerated for writing to his master's wife. His action in the letter indicated the commitment of a slave boy to protect his master's property and family. Unfortunately for Joiner, he was not so lucky when it came to the master's 18-year-old daughter. He lost his life at the hands of a white lynch mob and its so-called defender of the white women's pride. Meanwhile, Black women were not exempted from brutal and inhumane treatment by white lynch mobs. When the Klan and the Nightriders took the lead in terrorizing Blacks, their preferred means of punishment for Black women was whipping and lynching. Black women were often ordered to kneel on the ground and made to strip naked while being whipped by white Klan members.

Violence against Blacks was satanic, malicious, dark and brooding with malevolent intent in nature, and the Klan and the Nightriders' culture were galvanized to instill fear in the Black population of America and degrade them to a lowest-class human status. As the violence escalated, many Black families fled into nearby woods to hide from the violence of the white Klan members and local authorities who were themselves often Klan members. Unfortunately, many poor Blacks hiding out in the woods and nearby bushes experienced all manner of illnesses and starvation from hunger.

Meanwhile, as America's racial tensions became an issue of southern states, Northern states suffered as well. Abraham Lincoln and many Americans came to support the notion that American race relations could never be resolved. One possible solution advocated among the white elite class at a time when the assimilation of America black population into the American society seemed impossible was the complete separation of white and free black American. He argued and supported the idea that the American Black population should be repatriated back to Africa as a permanent solution to the racial tension in America.

Lincoln and other prominent Americans believed that the two races could never be made to live together in peace. Not only did Lincoln and the majority white population subscribe to the notion of Black repatriation to Africa, this notion was also held among many free Blacks and enslaved Blacks as well. For enslaved Blacks and free men of color, many had come to the sad conclusion that after centuries of building, dying, and suffering with the sweat and blood of their ancestors for the white man, all they had gotten back was the abject hatred and satanic, malicious treatment from the white population. For most of these acrimonious people of color, going back to Africa, a land they knew nothing about, was the best thing for American Blacks.

Prominent among the leading voices for the repatriation of America Blacks to Africa was led by Bishop Henry McNeal Turner, who was a leader in championing the crusade of free Black emigration to a Black homeland in Africa. Turner and others fully believed that no prominent future was assured for free Blacks in America. Turner a blunt forceful man who pushed his way into the ranks of the black Americans struggled, was also of the belief that perhaps God had it in His plan to introduce Blacks to Christianity through slavery, but he conceded that America had reneged on its part of God's plan by not allowing free men of color to integrate as full human beings and to become full flesh and blood citizens of the land that they were born in. Turner acknowledged that the next options were for Blacks to proceed with God's next big plan for them—emigrating back to Africa.

The Black American dream of emigrating to the motherland "Africa" had always been a long-held view by many free and enslaved Blacks. Their ancestors also held the view of repatriating back to the land where they were kidnapped and forcibly captured from early on. Some free men of color sold all their belongings to put down money as partial payment toward their emigration to Liberia when the country was founded as a permanent home for free Black Americans.

As early as 1787 in Newport, Rhode Island, a group of freemen of color organized the Free African Society, a group that encouraged other free Blacks to repatriate to Africa. In response to the organization's crusade, a wealthy Black businessman and shipowner name Paul Cuffee, who was of Ghanaian descent, took a group of freedmen of color to Africa free of charge in 1815. Unfortunately, the plan for a mass Black repatriation to Africa seemed to have been most popular with whites, particularly white abolitionists, then with Blacks themselves. In 1818 the American Colonization Society, created mostly by white abolitionists, succeeded in establishing a small colony for free Black Americans in Monrovia on the West African coast, which later became known as the Republic of Liberia.

CHAPTER 6

THE FOUNDING OF A BLACK AMERICAN HOMELAND

Photo by: Alvin L. Sieh

The founding of this small West African country called Liberia was not coincidental. The initial concept began early in the 1800s, the result of domestic politics surrounding slavery, economics and racial tension in the United States. Other factors that brought about the black colony creation were also influenced by American foreign policy interests. As the number of freed Blacks grew at an alarming rate for some in the white majority, the issues of citizenship rights, slavery, labor rights and a myriad of other social issues surrounding the Black and white races quickly became fodder of everyday discussion in American lives. These social issues affected every sphere of American society. Prominent Americans from each side of the discussion began to grandstand in the American political arena, with each side voicing its displeasure about race relations in the nation.

On one side of the debate were slaveholders and their supporters, while on the other side were the abolitionists made up of mostly Northerners. As pressure mounted from abolitionists and their prominent supporters regarding the welfare of America minority Black populations, an agreement was reached to resettle freedmen of color in Africa. Through a compromise agreement, the American Colonization Society was founded in 1816 with the blessing of U.S. president James Monroe and the U.S. Congress under his administration. Congress under Monroe provided funding in 1820 to enable the ACS to establish a black settlement that would later become the nation of Liberia on the west coast of the African continent as a black American homeland.

Liberia is surrounded by the Atlantic Ocean and bordered by Sierra Leone, Guinea and the Ivory Coast. The capital city Monrovia was named after President James Monroe as a gesture for his immense contribution in the creation of the country. Prominent among the supporters of establishing a Black American colony in Africa was Abraham Lincoln, who endorsed the idea that repatriating America Black populations back to Africa was the most sensible solution for America's racial dilemmas. While Lincoln lent his support to the repartition of free Black Americans to Africa, many historians believed that he did so in order to save the union, as racial tension and slavery were consuming the fabric of American society.

Lincoln described his true feelings about the issues of slavery and the rights of American Black people in his letter to Horace Greeley, editor of the New York Tribune. Lincoln wrote, "Dear sir, I have not meant to leave anyone in doubt that my paramount objective in this struggle is to save the union and is not either to save or destroy slavery. If I could save the Union without freeing any slave, I would do it, and if I could save it by freeing all the slaves, I would do it, and if I could do it by freeing some and leaving others alone, I would also do that. What I do about slavery and the colored race, I do because it helps to save this union, and what I forbear, I forbear because I do not believe it would help to save the union. I have here stated my purpose according to my view of official duty, and I intend no modification of my expressed personal wish that all men, everywhere, could be free. Yours, A. Lincoln."

Although Lincoln's personal view on the issue of slavery was clearly ambivalent, his official perceptions on the issue were unmistakably clear. Meanwhile, some prominent Blacks and white supporters of the abolitionist movement fundamentally dismissed the view that it was impracticable for the races to peacefully intermingle in one society. Opposition from these groups stood against the idea of supporting an African American settlement in Africa. Also, against the settlement of Black Americans to Africa were Southern planters and plantation owners. In the wake of the economic boom and demand in the cotton and indigo markets in the 1820s and the unyielding demand for free slave labor, Southern plantation owners vigorously mounted a campaign to discourage the notion of Black repatriation to Africa.

These Southerners were deeply worried about the potential economic loss to their booming cotton industry if Blacks caught on to the idea of repatriation. Meanwhile, slaveholders somehow succeeded in tamping down the enthusiasm among some Black Americans, which diminished support for repatriation to Africa for freedman of color. For some of them, the idea of returning to Africa flickered uncertainty in their minds. The cruel memories of being sold by other Black Africans to white slave traders, and being torn away from their languages, customs and traditions were traumatizing memories that caused many freedmen of color to view Africa as a dangerous place to resettle despite their horrible treatment in the land of their white masters.

For many Black Americans, however, the idea of settlement in Africa remained a sustaining hope for those who had come to strongly dislike the status quo. Meanwhile, the ACS had prominent supporters, both Black and white, who became astute in helping the resettlement issues gain momentum. In 1818 the ACS dispatched two of its members to West Africa in search of a suitable territory for the settlement of Black Americans. Upon the arrival of these two representatives on the Grain Coast, they were unable to persuade the local inhabitants and tribal leaders to sell them territory for the new Black colony. Un-deterred about the local tribal leaders' refusal to sell land to the ACS representatives, in 1820 eighty-eight free Black Americans, along with three members of the ACS, sailed for Sierra Leone in search of a territory to be used for the settlement.

Before the delegation departed for Africa, however, they were made to sign a constitution requiring that an agent of the ACS administer the new settlement under U.S. law. Upon the arrival of the ACS delegation in Sierra Leone, they found shelter on Scherbo Island off the west coast. However, conditions on the island were deemed unlivable for the newcomers. The island was known to be mosquito infested. Many of the delegates and settlers later died from malaria carried by the mosquitoes. News of the settlers' deaths reached the United States government in a bid for help.

In desperation to find a suitable settlement in Africa for the Black American settlers, a U.S. navy vessel in 1821 under the stewardship of Lieutenant Robert Stockton resumed the search for a permanent settlement in what is now known as the Republic of Liberia. Just as with the Americans before Robert Stockton, the local tribal leaders once again refused the second attempt to purchase land for the settlement of the freed Blacks. This time rather than taking no for an answer, the United States naval officer forced a local tribal leader at gunpoint to sell a strip of land to the ACS. With the purchase of the new settlement on the Grain Coast, the remaining survivors of the Scherbo Island delegation were relocated to the new colony on the coast.

With the new settlement under the authority of the ACS, it was later populated by other free Black Americans who later joined the original settlers when they heard of the creation of a Black American homeland in Africa. Even though it was under coercion that the native inhabitants of the Grain Coast relinquished their land to the Americans, they did not disappear quietly. Under cover of darkness, local tribes mounted fierce resistance against the new settlers. They attacked the settlers regularly, making it impossible for them to live in peace. Threatened by constant harassment from local inhabitants, in 1824 the Black American settlers erected fortifications around the colony for protection from outside attacks. That same year the new settlement was named Liberia representing the word liberty, which of course stood for the inhabitants' prized status.

As the ACS work and the new colony expanded, other colonization societies sponsored by individual states and wealthy philanthropists purchased land and relocated Black settlers near Monrovia the Liberian capital. Maryland Colony declared its independence from the Maryland State Colonization Society but did not become part of the Republic of Liberia. It held control of the coastal territories between the Grand Cess and San Pedro Rivers. American Blacks were not the only fortunate group to settle in the new colony. Other Black Africans captured from illegal US. and British slave ships by naval ships after abolition was passed were also settled in the colony. New settlers totaling in number almost 20,000 inhabitants did not integrate with native tribes. For the most part, they separated themselves from the natives, whom they considered savages and managed to maintain their imported American culture and ways of life.

The Black American settlers began forming a style of government mirroring that of the U.S. and they naturally looked toward the American government for financial support. However, their hopes were soon dashed when the U.S. government faced its own financial problems domestically and urged the new colony to move toward self-sufficiency. With financial support from the

United States government unavailable, the colony continued to deal with constant threats and intimidation from the British and French navies which persistently encroached upon its territories. Forced to defend its economic and security interests, the ACS urged the new Liberian government to declare its independence and become self-sufficient. Despite the uncertainty, the new colony was successful in establishing trade and commerce as it moved speedily toward self-sufficiency and self-government. Despite this, the proximity of the French and British troops off the African coast was viewed by the colony as a threat to its security and economic viability.

As a result, in 1847, Liberia declared her independence from the American Colonization Society in order to establish a sovereign nation and create its own commerce. The decision to declare independence did not sit well with many foreign factions, especially the British. Many British companies were affected by Liberia's decision to declare itself a sovereign nation. Despite protests from the British companies affected by the decision, the British government was the first foreign power to officially extend international recognition to the newly independent nation. In addition, in 1848 Britain took another step forward by entering a treaty of commerce with Liberia.

In the intervening period, when it came time for the United States government to recognize the independence of the Liberian nation that it helped established, it decided to stonewall the decision. Since it was the United States government that urged Liberia to move toward self-government, it is puzzling that it would refuse to recognize Liberia independence. However, some historians believe that America's refusal to recognize Liberia as an independent nation was driven by fear that it may have conflicted with slavery issues still very much alive in the United States. It would also disprove the racist and ignorance idea that Black Americans are unable to lead or administer self-governance.

The issue of slavery was still center stage in America's political discourse, even after the abolishment of the slave trade in 1808. The ACS came under intense scrutiny from American abolitionists, who alleged that the removal of free Black slaves from the United States emboldened the institution of slavery. Some abolitionists had an unassailable belief that Blacks, and white people were capable of coexisting in America as free citizens. Many freed Black Americans also shared that belief. Some of those freedmen also believed that Black Americans should be allowed to stay in America with the same rights as free white Americans.

In a freed Black gathering in New York in 1831, many of the participants looked toward the realization of true democracy in the United States of America for all Black people, believing that it was only a matter of time before God would hasten to their call. Some declared that the U.S. was their home and their country. Beneath its soil and dirt lay the bones of their forefathers—fathers, mothers, brothers and sisters. For America some of their forebears fought, bled and died. They were born in America, planned to die and be buried alongside their ancestors in America. Those very mixed feelings caused many freed Blacks to lose interest in abandoning their homes and birthplace in the United States for the west African country of Liberia.

However, between 1822 and the American Civil War, nearly 16,000 freed Black Americans were repatriated and eventually settled in Liberia. Meanwhile, after Great Britain's recognition of Liberia's independence France, Prussia, and Belgium followed by recognizing Liberia as well. Unfortunately for the free Black American settlers in Liberia, it would take nearly 15 years before the United States of America finally recognized and accepted the independence of Liberia, which was, ironically, a nation that came into being because of the very creation of America. The birth of the Liberian nation was an experiment in and of itself.

The idea for the creation of Liberia was initially put forward by wealthy philanthropists and politicians in America in order to address the nation's racial tension. It is unfortunate that both Black and white Americans did not build further on the success story that lead to the creation of the beautiful tropical country along the Atlantic Ocean, with its tremendous natural and human resources. Just like the Jewish people were able to redeem the state of Israel, today Jews from everywhere around the world, including non-Jews, are able to benefit from the investment, sacrifice, and talent of those pioneers who laid down their lives and wealth to make it the state it is today. Black Americans, including some white Americans, hold that same responsibility to redeem Liberia and make it the Promised Land it was meant to be for the America Black population, as well as a symbol of an experiment of American democracy everywhere around the world.

Meanwhile, on July 26, 1847 on the dark continent of Africa, a new nation was born, set up in the likeness of American democracy with three branches of government. Like the United States of America, Liberia has an executive branch headed by a president who is elected by the free will of the Liberian citizens through independent elections. The legislative branch's members are elected by the citizens of their respective counties and districts, and the judicial branch's members are appointed by the executive branch and controlled by the legislative branch. As in the United States, in Liberia each branch of the government is equal according to the Liberian constitution.

Remarkably for the Liberian nation, while many so-called advanced nations today struggle to rise from the dark ages, Black Americans who were largely considered unable to govern their own affairs were actually perfecting and working on a better democracy that America and the rest of the so-called civilized world knew nothing about. Some racist white people describe Black Americans and the Black race as a degenerate class in desperate need of white patronage in order to survive. Some were of the ignorant mindset that the Black race is handicapped without the white race teaching them about their own affairs. Some argued that the Black race would not survive or govern itself without carnage and bloodshed. They admonished that without the guidance of so-called white masters, the Black race was doomed. Contrary to this false belief among some ignorant people of the western world, including some of the brightest minds among them, the small Black nation of Liberia under difficult circumstances was at the time building a vibrant democracy mirroring that of the United States of America.

Freed Black Americans, or Americo Liberians, who were then running a functioning republic, self-ruled and self-guided 100% by freedmen of color, contradicted the prejudiced notions held by whites about the Black race. As Liberia progressed toward its independence and democracy, former slaves who were now freedmen of color began the building of institutions of learning, and cities and towns, using American designed architecture imported from America's southern states. These symbols can be seen today in many places in Liberia where the earlier Black Americans settled.

Black Americans also brought with them the American culture and social lifestyles which today have great influence on the culture and lifestyle of all Liberians. In those darker days, Black Americans also brought with them Christianity and helped build religious institutions. They organized social class systems and connections through organizations such as the Freemasons, and political parties such as the Republican party and the True Whig party. Free Blacks also built universities and colleges such as the College of West Africa which opened in 1839, making it one of the oldest European style schools in Africa. In 1889, Cuttington University, a private university in Suacoco was opened by the Episcopal Church of the United States. It is one of the known oldest private, co-educational four-year degree-granting institutions in sub-Saharan Africa.

As Liberia was laying its cornerstone around its infant democracy, back in the United States racial tension was at its peak during the latter part of the 18th century and the early part of the 19th century. Freed Blacks and newly emancipated slaves who, of their own accord, decided not to make the journey to Liberia, soon found themselves in the crossfire of America's great racial epoch known as the Civil War.

After the American Civil War, the period lasting between 1865 to 1877 is considered among historians as one of the most twisted and sickening periods of American racial tension. It was in this era that the white majority thwarted and derailed Black America's growing aspirations for economic prosperity and full rights to citizenship. In nearly every corner of American society, many whites presented strong resistance and violent reactions against freed Blacks as a means of quashing their aspirations for financial and economic security as well as full equal rights in the United States.

Powerful factions in the American South were determined to return the nation to its prewar era, where black Americans were considered the property of white masters and plantation owners and held in bondage. The Northerners were prudent and concise in their determination not to allow the nation to leapfrog back into its pre-war status quo, and they fought tenaciously to make certain that the status of freed Black Americans remained front and center in political and cultural debates.

Sadly, for anti-slavery and abolitionist supporters, the federal government's position on the status of Black Americans was unsteady and gloomy. The government took an inconspicuous position of not getting involved with issues of slavery, which it considered a "southern affair of property." Due to the undefined federal will on the issue of slavery, southern states in large numbers-controlled citizens' political and legal rights and resisted the exigency to administer any federal laws that dealt with the issues of slavery or Black American equal rights.

In the wake of the federal government's lack of willpower to vigorously champion the issues of citizenship rights for Black Americans, the issue leaned on the half-century-old argument brought forward by Northern abolitionists who fostered the debate that national citizenship was a privilege that should be enjoyed equally by whites and Blacks as a national right. They also asserted that it was the responsibility of the federal government to enforce those ideas that were the cornerstones of the nation's founding.

The abolitionists' argument is supported by the thirteenth amendment of the Constitution, which abolished slavery, and the fourteenth amendment guaranteeing equal rights and protection before the law, including the right to due process for all Americans, including Black Americans (but not Native American Indians at that time). The fifteenth amendment attempted to address the rights of freed Blacks, allowing them to vote in national and local elections. The dominant forces in American society in the last quarter of the 18th century and through the early part of the 19th century were social and economic issues addressing the rights of the people.

During the economic and social anxiety also taking place at the end of the 18th century, the federal government was steadily increasing its power, moving carefully to enforce certain laws and pass new sweeping ones. In an effort by the federal government to protect the rights of all citizens, including Blacks, the Reconstruction Act of 1867 and the 1870s Enforcement Acts, expanded the federal government's authority to uphold and protect all citizens' constitutional rights under the law.

As new federal laws began to recognize the rights of Black Americans, many of them took it upon themselves to learn how to read and write, as it was no longer forbidden for them to do so. However, the culture of slavery was not emboldened to educate or prepare its former slaves for self-preservation. Black American slaves who emancipated from the bondage of the slaves' hegemony had a crippling lack of education and technical skills that would have prepared them to integrate into the emerging economic prosperity of the post-war nation.

In its attempt to address the issues of freed Blacks, the federal government created the Bureau of Refugees, Freedmen and Abandoned Lands through an act of Congress in March of 1865. The Freedmen's Bureau's initial role was to assist the nearly four million newly freed Black American citizens, most of whom were from former Confederate states. The Freedmen's Bureau, under the stewardship of Otis Oliver Howard, assisted in opening several Black schools, including the first all-Black colleges, such as the Hampton Institute, Atlanta University, Howard University, and Fisk University. In addition, the Freedmen's Bureau also enacted health and social services to encourage freed Blacks to be active in the democratic process by voting and through political participation.

The Bureau made many earnest attempts under Oliver Howard to help provide for the needs of many freed Blacks who were displaced as a result of the American Civil War. In one of its daring moves, the Freemen's Bureau seized former plantation land. This lionhearted effort on the part of the Bureau was geared toward rewarding former slaves, most of whom had worked and lived more than half their lives on those seized plantations. The Bureau divided the land among freed Black slaves to live and farm on. The land distribution came to be known as the "Forty Acres and a Mule" deal, ordered at the end of the war by General Sherman, although the land was never bequeathed to freed slaves and was ultimately returned to its original white owners.

Meanwhile, as the Bureau was making tremendous strides in the resettlement efforts of freed Black Americans under the stewardship of Otis Howard, there were those who were working expeditiously to undermine his reform efforts. Inundated with resentment from former Confederate states, and the widespread lack of interest for freed Black American citizenship, along with a lack of sponsorship by President Andrew Johnson and some Northern congressional leaders, the Bureau's reform efforts were brought to a standstill. President Johnson dealt a final blow to the Bureau's ambitious reform efforts when he stripped away the Bureau's land redistribution initiatives, allowing that land to be returned to the original Southern plantation owners. For most freed Blacks in America, Johnson's action was viewed as outrageous and disgraceful.

Black Americans felt betrayed that the chance to own land in America was abandoned by the very government that was supposed to guarantee that the nearly four million freed Blacks were officially part of the country they'd lived and died for over a period of 300 years. The foundation of American wealth building was guaranteed by the ability to own land. This was underscored by the fact that only landowners could vote. It was no wonder then that German immigrant and journalist Carl Schurz noted that Black Americans saw possession of land as the ultimate "consummation of their deliverance." With few rights and little to no recognition, free Black Americans found themselves in a de facto system of slavery.

Even though slavery was legally abolished in all the former Confederate states, most freed Blacks were apprehensive of their former slave masters, most fearing that they could be forced back into bondage. At the same time, sensing the demise of the Freedmen's Bureau, powerful and corrupt white politicians and white plantation owners took advantage of the fact that most free Blacks were illiterate. In fact, only about one in ten freed Black slaves could read or write. For those who could, they did so by violating laws forbidding them to read or write.

Many freed Blacks were made to sign dubious contracts that forced them into unjust labor obligations to white planters. Nearly every state could enact laws governing the behavior of freed Black Americans, which were enforced in most cases. A southern code of conduct called the "Black Code" was instituted. The code restricted the movement of freed Blacks, and prohibited plantation owners from attempting to entice Black laborers away from existing work with the enticement of better conditions and pay.

The law also empowered white planters to put Black children to work who appeared to not have any corroborative financial support or care. These children were put alongside adults in fields doing work they were not physically mature enough to perform. The law also prohibited Blacks from owning and possessing guns. They were also not permitted to testify in a court proceeding against a white person (which permitted crimes against Blacks to proliferate). Every form of intermarriage was also prohibited.

Without the right to land ownership, freed Black Americans were forced to enter into new contracts agreement with white planters. The new labor practice came to be called "sharecropping." The sharecropping agreement allotted the croppers a small piece of land to work on, a modest house, seed, water, and other essential needs such as tools and crude furniture. There was also typically a small patch of land to grow their own food and gardens. At the end of the planting season the sharecroppers received payments from the sale of cotton crops, the proceeds of which were divided between the owner and the sharecropper after expenses are subtracted by the owner.

The sharecropping arrangement did not help the workers financially in any significant way; this one-sided arrangement only helped white planters to amass more wealth at the expense of the sweat and labor of the freed Black Americans working their lands. Most historians describe the sharecropping arrangement as slavery of a different kind. The sharecropping arrangement was one-sided, and the planters and landowners had all the advantages, including selling the crops at market. The croppers did not have this right. As a result, Black sharecroppers were forced to take the word of the white planters as to the final selling price of the crops at market. Often, planters and plantation owners were not forthcoming about the true value or final price of the crops when it came to giving the Black croppers their fair share of the sales.

Most Black croppers, however, resided on the planter's land and often received items or services that were not included in the basic work arrangement. Because of the Black croppers paying back money to the owners for services provided, when it came time to share the proceeds or profit, the Black croppers were often left with nothing for the entire crop season. Under this apartheid arrangement, Black Americans had no hope of economic prosperity as they sank into a cycle of abject poverty and endless servitude. For these freed Black Americans fighting for the right to own property in America, life became extremely difficult under President Johnson and Reconstruction. Freed Black American advancement in America after emancipation was rife with ongoing struggles, with no end in sight.

The odds were against freed Blacks in every aspect of American society. However, despite their poor conditions and treatment in the United States along with systematic racial persecution and continued violence at the hands of white Americans, many Black Americans were still unwilling to resettle in Liberia. News of their brethren dying of disease, famine and constant skirmishes with the natives was unsettling for most Black Americans, and they decided against making the journey to Liberia.

For those free Black Americans who made the earlier journey, they were able to settle in and become builders of a new nation in Africa, completing a long-held dream by enslaved Blacks of returning to their motherland. By the year 1870, Liberia had attracted nearly 14,000 former Black American slaves from the United States. Migration to Liberia by Black Americans dramatically decreased after 1870. However, freed Blacks from the U.S. and the Caribbean Islands continued to arrive in Liberia sporadically over time.

In the United States, despite the abolishment of slavery after the Civil War and the defeat of the Confederate States of America, freed Black Americans mostly in southern states continued to be at a disadvantage in every aspect of American life. Frederick Douglass best explained the free Black American condition in his book, *The Life and Times of Frederick Douglass*. Douglass wrote that although no longer a slave, the Black American suffered intolerable conditions and treatment, compelled to work for whatever an employer pleased to pay, swindled out of hard earnings by money orders redeemed in stores, compelled to pay the price of an acre of ground for its use during a single year, paying four times more than a fair price for a pound of bacon, and kept upon the narrowest margin between life and starvation.

For most Black Americans, although no longer legally slaves in America, all the conditions of segregation and racial inequality applied to them in the country of their birth. During the Reconstruction years, Black Americans still endured inequality in the court system, and constant harassment and violence from whites. Often this violence resulted in mob lynching, murder, torture or burning at the cross for public viewing.

Unfortunately, these and other violent acts against Black Americans continued unabated for decades until the advent of the civil rights movement of the 1960s, when the issues of segregation and American racism were made front page discussions in public squares. The civil rights movement forced recognition of the differences between right and wrong regarding the plight of Black American citizens who had long been ignored and denied the right of first-class citizenship in their nation of birth. However, despite federal government programs and equal opportunity laws that abolished discrimination in education, housing, property ownership, and employment, Black Americans remained unequal partners with their white counterparts in American society.

Before the mid-1960s, the civil rights movement was driven by competing interest groups from across all sections of American society, largely consisting of middle-class Americans. The movement adopted a non-violence and passive resistance approach to change discrimination laws and practices, primarily in the southern states of the U.S. Until the civil rights achievements and advancements and the 1964 adoption of the Civil Rights Act, most southern Black Americans found it impossible to exercise their voting rights. Mass demonstrations were held in 1965 to challenge the violence and other segregation and racial means used by whites to prevent Black Americans from voter registration.

One of the well-documented demonstrations started in Selma, Alabama, which began as a peaceful march before turning violent when white authorities attempted to break it up. In its aftermath, the Johnson administration responded with the Voting Rights Act of 1965, which abolished the literacy test that white authorities were imposing on Black voters, along with other voter restrictions.

Under President Lyndon Johnson's administration, the wheels of the civil rights movement went into a spin when he moved to authorize federal government intervention against voter discrimination at the hands of white authorities and pollsters. As the result of removing barriers that made it hard for Black Americans to vote, those who had not been allowed to vote in the past began to come out in waves in order to exercise their new voting rights. Meanwhile, the rise in Black American voters transformed politics in southern states tremendously. Despite the legislative gains, many Black Americans saw the civil rights movement as having been too slow to deal with the centuries-old oppression and denial that Black Americans had endured.

As many Black Americans became dissatisfied with the slow progress of the civil rights revolution, the movement was challenged by the Black Power movement. Many Black supporters and advocates of the civil rights movement saw the Black Power movement as a better force to address the urgent needs of Black American despair. However, the policies of Black Power lead to some members feeling alienated and left out. This eventually put a crippling dent in the civil rights revolution. As a result of competing policy agendas, many white supporters of the civil rights movement shied away from the movement's activities.

Race riots soon followed the change in strategies and competing ideologies between the Black Power movement and supporters of the civil rights revolution. In Los Angeles and some of the nation's largest cities, violence broke out in 1965 as race tensions flared up. In the Watts district of Los Angeles, 34 people lost their lives in the violence. Nearly two years later, Detroit and Newark were the incubators of other race riots that left entire neighborhoods ruined by death and the destruction of property.

Riots in American cities abated after the tragic assassination of Dr. Martin Luther King Jr. in April of 1968. Similarly, in Liberia the indigenous majority population were not allowed the right of citizenship in their own country. It would take nearly a century and a half and the assassination of a president for the Liberian constitution to finally recognize the native majority as citizens in their own land.

CHAPTER 7

THE MISEDUCATION OF LIBERIAN NATIVES

Photo by: Alvin L. Sieh

After the freed American slaves landed in 1822 at what is now Liberia, they began to create a government resembling that of the USA. They also established a system of segregation and suppression of the native Liberian majority, who ironically had given them their blessing to settle on their land. After independence was achieved in 1847, former Virginian and Petersburg Joseph Jenkins Robert, who was born a freedman in Norfolk, Virginia, became its first president. A native of Virginia, J.J. Robert was the son of free black whose heritage was more than seven- eighths white. He worked with his stepfather on a flatboat on the James River. Robert gained his early education by reading books from the private library of William Colson, a black barber under whom he apprenticed.

At 20 years old he immigrated to Liberia with his mother and younger brothers. He became a successful merchant and an unofficial aide to the white governor of the colony, Thomas H Buchanan, a member of the American Colonization Society, which sought the return of American freedmen to Africa. Upon Thomas Buchanan's death in 1842, J.J Robert was appointed the first black governor of the colony. He was also a military commander and possessive a great diplomatic skill and an ambitious freed man of his time. He was often admired for his great public speaking skills.

An excerpt from J.J Robert's inaugural address compares with all the great minds and orators of both past and present, some of whom have been quoted and admired by great speakers of our time. J.J. Robert was born at a time in America when Black Americans lacked educational opportunities. No doubt he, along with many other freed Black Americans, grew up in an oppressed environment rife with obstacles to gaining an education.

In his inaugural speech, President Robert said, "When we look abroad and see by what slow and painful steps, marked with blood and ills of every kind, other states of the world have advanced to liberty and independence, we cannot but admire and praise that all gracious providence, who by his unerring ways, has with so few sufferings on our part compared with other states, led us to this happy stage in our progress toward those great and important objects. He will miraculously make Liberia a paradise and deliver us in a moment from all the ills and inconvenience consequent upon the peculiar circumstances under which we are placed."

In his speech, Robert understood the long journey that African Americans traveled and the sacrifices they made to finally achieve the long-held dream of enslaved Africans—for the opportunity to self-govern in their own land. If readers break down his speech and reflect on the torment and suffering of Black Americans and their journey back to their ancestral land, you would have to honestly agree that he deserves a place among great speakers and orators, past or present.

Meanwhile, as Black Americans began forming communities in Monrovia, many of them resented the native people, who were the majority population. They were viewed as being primitives and savages, just another ugly lesson that they learned and imported into Liberia from their former slave masters in America. Similarly, in America when the early Europeans settlers could not get their way with the Native American Indians, they referred to them as primitives and savages. Ironically, all the ideas that brought about the founding of Liberia and its institutions of government did not recognize the existence of native-born Liberians.

Their existence was not mentioned in its constitution or the early documents of the nation. Strangely, the freed Black American who settled in Liberia had the very same mindset as the earlier settlers of the United States of America. White European settlers did not mention or include the Native American Indians in the founding document of the nation. They were determined to establish a nation for the white race only. However, due to many freed slaves in the nation, and their inability to repatriate all the Blacks back to Africa, Black Americans were later included in the US Constitution.

Flash forward to Liberia, where the Black American settlers purposely excluded the native-born Liberians from the founding document and affairs of the Liberian nation. It is mind-boggling that a group of people once persecuted and oppressed for so long because of their race and the differences from their oppressors, would intentionally travel to a place far away from their oppressors, only to end up becoming the oppressors to those who welcomed them. There is a precept that says, "The oppressed always become the oppressors." The early settlers in America were escaping oppression perpetrated on them by the massive British Empire. Upon arriving on the shore of North America as settlers they turned on the native inhabitants and became the oppressors of the Native American Indians and later oppressors of Black Africans whom they imported as slaves to work their fields and plantations.

In Liberia, Black American settlers discriminated and distanced themselves from the native Liberians. Not much is known about the level of education of the settlers at the time; however, they viewed the native Liberians as uncivilized, illiterate beings and they wanted nothing to do with them. In their arrogance, they denied the existence of the native Liberians. They omitted any mention of them in the Liberian Declaration of Independence by the following passages, "We, the people of Liberia, were originally inhabitants of the United States of North America." In this passage, the Black American settlers were only mentioning themselves, not the native Liberians.

As a result of the mistreatment and exclusion of the native Liberians in the new colony, the natives were in a state of constant rebellion against the Black American settlers. The rebellion was supported by a local chief named Grando, who was opposed to the indoctrination of western culture and civilization upon his people. Despite his opposition to the western culture of the Black American settlers, the chief did not mind transacting business with the settlers' administration, which was controlling Monrovia. Grando sold a tract of land to the new settlers and received payment with his signature. He later returned, demanding the land back without returning the payment. The chief had always acted rogue since the arrival of the Black American settlers. He kept the Bassa tribe in a constant state of hostility toward the settlers and their administration in Monrovia. Unfortunately for the Black American settlers, the Bassa tribes were not the only native tribes to feel antipathy about their settlement. The settlers encountered other native tribes around the coastal areas of Liberia that were suspicious and hostile toward them.

As the new settlers' administration began to take shape with the exclusion of the native-born Liberians, English automatically became the official language of the new nation. The English language was, of course, foreign to the indigent Liberians, making it difficult if not impossible to intermingle with the Black American settlers. The settlers established a one-party system of government known as the True Whig party; a name imported from the United States. Though the new Liberian constitution drafted by the settlers was democratic in form, in practice it was a one-party system that was mostly autocratic in principle. The need for two parties or a multi-party democracy was not considered by the settlers, partly because they were the only ones who could vote and participate in politics or the governing affairs of the nation.

For Liberian American former slaves, establishing a colony in Africa was a way to escape white racism, violence, and oppression. The idea that they were going to share their established colony with the natives, some of whom were violent and threatening toward them, was certainly not under consideration. In 1862, according to historian Nat Gararea Gbessagee, the Liberian Supreme Court ruled in a unanimous decision that the natives were nothing more than subjects of the state who were required to abide by the laws of the Republic of Liberia, but not entitled to the privilege of citizenship. This was because they were considered incapable of understanding the inner workings of the government. In retrospect, the same arguments were made in America about Black Americans in some early documents of the nation's founding. However, one wonders why a group of people like the Black Americans denied the very basic right of citizenship to others in that land who were native born—whose ancestors bled, sweat and died—and who would be cognizant of the injustice against themselves and other groups. Most would think the Black American newcomers would be meticulously mindful of not subjecting others to the same exclusions they suffered in North America.

Ironically in the U.S., certain states prohibited Black American schoolchildren from knowing certain passages of the Declaration of Independence. Black Americans in some states were not allowed to use schoolbooks in which the Declaration of Independence was printed. They were not allowed to learn that one of the founding fathers, Thomas Jefferson, believed that government should derive its power from the consent of the people. Proponents of denying Black youth from knowing the constitutional protection of liberty and freedom for all Americans regardless of race or creed, were shamefully wrong.

Early historians writing about Liberia discarded the importance of the native-born Liberians. Early writings were based on propaganda and willful ignorance of the early cultures of the indigenous diverse tribes and people of the Pepper Coast. It is safe to say that the goal of these early writers, most of whom came from the privileged class, were to purposefully present a biased point of view of the establishment of the Liberian nation. Unfortunately for the indigenous people, they did not have a system of writing down their accounts of the early history of their land. For these underdeveloped native tribes, their descendants were subjected to the biased, inaccurate accounts of propagandists, whose language of the history of Liberia is the only account recorded. These naive writers of history purposefully contended that the natives had not the ability or intellect to be civilized, and therefore lacked the reasoning to understand Black Americans' way of life, which was Western and thus foreign to the natives.

In their ignorance of the native history, the Black American settlers failed to realize that before their arrival in Liberia, the native tribes were organized and had a system of governance and trade that was functioning much like any civilization at the time. It is important to note that civilization is a normal acceptable way of life within a given society. While we created different kinds and different eras of civilization throughout the history of the world, we certainly do not hold the authority to scorn one civilization in order to give rise to another. As such, the native inhabitants of the coastal area prior to the arrival of the free Black Americans, had developed a monetary exchange system that worked among the various tribes. The coastal inhabitants traded extensively with the early settlers who visited the areas well before the arrival of the Black Americans.

While it is true that the civilization imported from America was new to the natives, declaring that the natives were uncivilized and lacked understanding of the functioning of government was ignorant and demeaning to many of the native tribes. Unfortunately, the Black American settlers did not understand that a fully functioning society worked only when its people are free to participate in the affairs of the nation. Any nation that excludes the participation of certain sections of its population, particularly the majority population, is a nation heading for abject failure. Perhaps the Black American settlers did not have the intellect to perceive that Liberia was on its way to becoming a failed state.

The United States of America slowly and painfully learned from its own mistakes when it realized that excluding a large percentage of its population from the affairs of governance and citizenship was tantamount to losing its place as a world power. It cost America a civil war, millions of lives and the destruction of property to rewrite her tormented history of cultural segregation and racial exclusion.

The Black American settlers missed a great opportunity by not embracing the national initiatives and cultural richness of the indigenous people of Liberia during the establishment of the nation. Perhaps the most corrosive results of this policy of segregation are the enduring consequences of the vibrant loss and brain-drain of the vast human resources and talent the native tribes could have contributed to the creation of the new nation of Liberia. Out of American ignorance of cultural inclusion and the acceptance of native culture, richness, cultural diversity, trade, tradition and customs of the native inhabitants were ignored.

Instead of incorporating and embracing the civilization and customs of their ancestors, Black Americans came to abhor and shy away from the cultural richness of their ancestors. One can only attribute their distaste and eschewing of the African culture and customs to their miseducation and enslavement in the land of their slave masters, where they were made to erase every aspect of their African culture. Liberia had a unique cultural diversity that could have been harnessed and made into the cultural epicenter where African civilization and Western civilization joined for social and economic growth for the whole of Africa to adopt and display. Liberia was fortunate to escape the ruthless hands of colonization and rampant exploitation, unlike many of her neighboring states that were held back by its oppressive grip.

In the mid-18th century after independence, Liberia was uniquely positioned to steer the wheels of prosperity, education and intellectual enlightenment for all its citizens and the African continent. Liberia had natural and human resources that could have been galvanized and nurtured for the uplifting of all its people. The 19ᵗʰ century could have seen Liberia among the world's most prosperous and advanced nations, both then and today.

It is heartbreaking, then, that the Black American settlers, along those who came after them, chose to sequester the opportunity to interconnect with the native majority and embrace their African culture and customs. The fact that Liberia isn't mentioned as a top destination in Africa or the world, where western culture imported by free American slaves interbred with native African culture for the uplifting of mankind is perplexing, especially since the free Black American slaves endured suffering and persecution for the opportunity to bring the two cultures together.

It is my opinion that the Black American settlers never considered the importance of educating the native majority population to a level where they could become scholars, entrepreneurs, inventors, scientists, agriculturalists, and archaeologists. Their lack of interest in the natives' education extended into the 20ᵗʰ century when they slowly began integrating with the native populations.

The educational system they built was not intended to empower the native population about the beauty of the African discovery of science, technology, medicine, trade, agriculture, literature, folklore, and the advance of social culture that kept the various tribal societies intrinsically interconnected. With the arrival of the western slave traders came the exploitive colonial powers that later replaced the slave trade with a new form of cruelty and swindling of the African continent's resources.

As a result of this distorted education, Africans who were educated by the inferior western educational system looked down upon their parents and relatives, who struggled to support their educational goals after working the fields all day. Rather than learning how to turn their family crops into an industry, they chose to learn other trades that would make them unemployed and even if they did manage to gain employment, they couldn't adequately apply the knowledge learned because the school curriculum was designed for western societies, not African societies.

For example, a social worker learning about social issues from an American, British or Belgium curriculum, would find those same theories could not be equally applied to resolve the social or economic issues facing a poor family in Liberia, Sierra Leone, or Guinea. A different set of studies and solutions are required to address those issues based on the politics, culture and customs of each country. The acknowledgment by former Liberian president Ellen

Johnson Sirleaf that "the Liberian educational system is a mess," underscores the point that the system was designed to miseducate native Liberians.

We should seriously reflect on our history to learn how our educational system became "a mess," and avoid continuing the outdated system of miseducating our children and limiting their participation in world advancement. As mentioned before, when the Liberian education system was designed by the Black American settlers, they never considered the idea of extending educational opportunities to the native population. It is safe to say that the educational system in Liberia was never intended for the indigenous people.

The settlers later incorporated the Congo people into their educational system as a way of extending influence and power over land and the native population. The Congo people of Liberia were originally slaves from the Republic of Congo, which was then called Congo Brazzaville. However, after the British and other western nations abolished the trans-Atlantic slave trade, there were still rogue westerners who clandestinely engaged in this illegal practice. Most of the illegal slave trade came into North America, as that country's demand for wealth building and free slave labor proliferated. It took America nearly 50 years before actually enforcing the ban on illegal slave commerce.

During this time, illegal African slaves from the Congo were rescued on the high seas by the British and French navies and brought to Liberia to settle with free Blacks. Since Liberia was already a new settlement for freed Black slaves from America, it was most convenient for nations to resettle the newly freed Congolese slaves there. Under control of the free Black American administration in Liberia, the rescued Congolese slaves became the largest group of native Africans to intermingle with the American settlers. The actual numbers of rescued Congolese are not known, but they are believed to be in the hundreds. The Black Americans became much more trusting and receptive to the Congolese settlers than to the native inhabitants in Liberia. Since Black American settlers were outnumbered by the native populations of Liberia and were constantly under some sort of harassment from some of them, it was in their best interest to quickly integrate the Congolese settlers, which they controlled, into Liberian society.

Black American settlers were also aware of their weakness in terms of sheer numbers. The American founding fathers' dream of exporting every freed Black from America to the new colony did not go over well, as many freed Blacks in the United States resented the idea of leaving the land that they and their ancestors helped build. Their forefathers bled, died and were buried on American soil, they argued, and they were not leaving it for a place they barely knew.

There were also other factors behind the slow migration to Liberia by American Blacks. There is no doubt that politics and economics were driving factors behind the slow migration to Liberia. However, the arrival of the rescued Congolese slaves in Liberia presented an opportunity for the Black American settlers to grow their numbers and power.

Congolese settlers were important as domestic servants and laborers for the Black American settlers. Unlike the freed Black American settlers who only spoke English, the Congolese slaves spoke different vernaculars and could often not communicate with each other because they came from different parts of Congo Brazzaville. Therefore, the Black settlers needed to ensure that the native Africans spoke the language of their former slave masters, a language that only they understood and spoke on the African continent. The rescued Congolese were also eager to learn and to adapt to the culture of their new hosts. The new settlers, despite being on the African continent, were themselves forcibly removed from their homeland and brought to a place they had no connection other than the skin color of the people that they were forced to resettle among. However, for the Congolese people to be able to integrate with the Black American settlers, cultural centers, schools and churches were built to educate and assimilate them into the new society.

As the Congolese settlers slowly melted into the Black American culture, the Black settlers took a lesson from the playbook of their former slave masters and applied it to the Congo settlers. Since they could not pronounce the native sounding African names of the Congo people, they went on to change the names of their Congolese domestic servants to their own first and last names. The Black Americans were able to change the names of their domestic servants to more English- and American-sounding names. The name changes did not end with the Congo people; they were later extended to the native inhabitants, who later became domesticated as servants and farm laborers to the Congo people who were by then in higher places in Liberian society.

In those days up to quite recently, an African-sounding name in Liberia was an indication of social class or level of education. If for example, you had an African- or native-sounding name, you were considered illiterate and you would most likely not get an opportunity for certain jobs or even marry a woman with an English-sounding name or a so-called Congo man's daughter. "You're not going to marry a countryman," was a common saying of the Congo elite in Liberia, referring to the native-born. So, to wed a Congo man's daughter, you had to have an English- or American-sounding name to stand a chance. These were the social, political and economic factors that led to most Liberians trading their African names for English-sounding names, such as Johnson, Peterson, Washington, Elwood, Williams, Dunn, Royce, Henderson, etc.

However, as time elapsed, the resettled Congolese people were absorbed into the low level of the freed Black American culture stage through education and cultural assimilation, and they eventually emerged as one group, making it harder to distinguish one group from the other. Through cultural consciousness, education, and inter-marriage between the two social classes, many barriers were removed, which allowed the Congos to move up to the Liberian upper class.

Congolese people could buy land, work, vote and run for elected offices in government. Since Monrovia was the governmental seat of the country, and later became the commercial and official capital of the Liberian government, almost all the land and properties were owned by the free settlers and upper-class Congo elites. The indigenous Liberians were excluded from all these affairs during the development of modern Liberia.

As Liberia developed and become a magnet for free and oppressed African and Caribbean people escaping colonial domination, tyranny, apartheid, economic injustice other forms of political oppression, Africans from Ghana, Nigeria, and Sierra Leone and the Caribbean successfully melted into the new Liberian culture that was deeply influenced by Western ways of life. Since most of these newcomers had some level of education to their credit, they easily blended in with the Congolese, who were now controlling key positions in the Liberian political and economic enclaves.

Most of the newly immigrated Africans settled with the Congolese and shared their culture and customs, most of which were adopted from the Americo Liberians. Some of these immigrant Africans became business owners, doctors, and educators.

CHAPTER 8

MISUSE OF CAPITAL BY LIBERIAN LEADERS

Due to intermarriage and reproduction between the descendants of Americo Liberian and the Congolese elite class, a minority ruling class emerged as the visibility of Black American descendants receded. With total control of the economic, political and social affairs of the nation, they were able to squander the nation's resources and capital by transferring government funds into personal overseas bank accounts and businesses abroad.

Over time, this new generation of leaders were able to build homes, compounds, and commercial buildings, gladly using money appropriated from national coffers. As they steadily built wealth, the ruling class shared important land and property among themselves. As for important lands that were owned by illiterate natives, they were forced to sell their real estate for little or nothing, based on fictitious laws or citations that the ill-educated natives did not understand.

For example, my late father, Sekou Kamara, was a professional tailor. In the early 1930s, he was a tailor and a vendor in Monrovia, the capital city. He was the unfortunate victim of an unjust land grab by the Congo ruling class. He owned land on what is now Randal Street, one of the most popular commercial streets in Monrovia. He had owned the land for a long time after purchasing it from one of the indigenous tribe members from that region. While visiting with us in Monrovia from the village of Old Korma, where he resided at the time before his death, my father and I were walking after visiting some friends in downtown Monrovia and we walked past a beautiful storefront with a display of imported furniture. He stopped abruptly and stared deeply at the furniture in the store with his eyes nearly invisible.

From the inside the store where all the beautiful well-made furniture was showcased, a Lebanese man and his wife sat with two Black men and a woman, who appeared to be the store attendants. They looked back at my father, confused. What was becoming a staring competition quickly ended when two of the Black store attendants approached my father and told him, "Old man you cannot place your hands on the glass window." The other man asked, "Papay," (a Liberian term for old man), "do you have money to buy something from this store?" My father did not respond to their questioning, but he quietly removed his palms from the window glass, leaving palm prints behind which caused an angry glance from the Black store attendant.

We were not there to buy any of their furniture, and besides, my father could not afford anything from the store. As he stepped back and began to walk away, I quietly and swiftly followed behind him, watching as he placed his hands behind his back, mimicking his signature trick. He always walked with his hands resting behind him, one holding the other from flapping.

As we walked away far from the store, my father told me about how the land the store sat on was forcibly taken away from him. "One day, a bigshot who was short with a big belly and a shiny bald head approached me in the store. His eyes looked like they were possessed by evil. The man stepped out of his black Mercedes Benz with two police officers guarding him. He ordered the two officers to give me and my family a letter. The man said that the letter was from the Ministry of Justice. I did not know what was in the letter because I could not read; the big short man asked another man dressed in a black suit to read the letter to me. After reading the letter, my father admitted that he did not understand any of the legal wording or court information. In a nation where the laws are written only in English and nearly 80% of the people cannot read or write, it was not strange for my father to be among the illiterate who did not understand the affairs of government.

After the man read the court letter to my father, my father told me that the only word that he understood from the whole confusion was when the so-called bigshot raised his voice and said: "You countryman .. you have two days to pack up and leave this place, or you will go to jail, this place now belongs to me." In those days, the native majority stood no chance of taking a Congolese person to court. The court belonged to the Congolese people, and they had learned its inner workings and processes from their adopted counterparts, the Americo Liberians, or Black Americans. So, for my father, the best chance he had to the best of his understanding was to pack up and abandon his land and building, so that was what he did.

Not understanding any of the historical context of the relationship between the native indigenous people and the so-called Congolese people, I asked my father, "Why did you give this place away? Do you know how much money you could be making from this place today?" Meanwhile, he went on to tell me unhurriedly about his terrifying experience with this so-called bigshot who came to tell him to walk away from his land or go to jail.

Amazingly, to my surprise, my father did not appear to be at all angered as he detailed his encounter. Unfortunately for him, the memories of that sad day would reappear after nearly 60 years when he came to live with his son briefly in Monrovia. For him, it had been way too long for him to be angry. As for me, I was fuming with anger. I knew the reason that the so-called Congolese people were wealthier than the indigenous majority was partly because of the grab-and-force seizure techniques they used to take away land from the natives. No doubt we would not have grown up poor if my father's land were not forcibly taken away from him.

The area where my father claimed his land was located is now developed with modern buildings and storefronts that are mostly owned by the ruling Congo elites and leased mostly to Lebanese and Indian merchants. However, my father was still able to recognize the area despite all the modern development. While I was seized by anger, for the most part my father was mesmerized by the transformation of the whole area. As we walked by different places he would stop and tell me stories of how he and his friends used to go hunting in the area. When my father told me these stories, I was in middle school and keenly aware of the history of how the ruling Congo class exploited the natives using laws and regulations that the native had no understanding of. I was deeply troubled by how the Congo ruling class used the nation's money through corruption and bribery to enrich themselves to the detriment of the poor illiterate masses that were mostly excluded from the affairs of the government.

Meanwhile, the homes, buildings, compounds, and lands bought with stolen money from the Liberian government coffers were leased or rented back to the Liberian government to use as ministries, agencies and other functions of the Liberian government. Until recently, nearly all of the ministries and agencies, including buildings such as the Ministry of Defense, justice, education, internal affairs and the Ministry of Finance, along with numerous other buildings were owned by the ruling Congolese elite class or other corrupt government officials.

Growing up in Liberia, as I began to dive into my country's history and ugly past, I was exposed to the wrong done to the native inhabitants who made up the majority of Liberia's population, first by the freed black American settlers and then by the Congolese slaves who later became the ruling class with the blessing of the freed Black Americans who accepted and educated them and later integrated them into their families. In my yearning to learn about my country's past, I soon discovered that most of my countrymen were uninformed about this deeply hidden history. The ignorance of my fellow countrymen about their country's past was not a willful failure of their own making, but rather it was designed to keep the native inhabitants and their generation ignorant of the country's past.

Growing up, most of the history I saw about Liberia started with the arrival of the freed Black Americans, whom our history books referred to as pioneers. This self-glorifying account detailed how a woman named Matilda Newport, who was an Americo Liberian colonist, became a folk hero. She is known for her actions in 1822 when she is alleged to have defended the settlement of Cape Mesurado by using her pipe to light cannon to fire against the advancing native Liberian inhabitants. Since then, the historical accuracy of her so-called heroic role has been challenged. A national holiday, a school and a popular street were named in her honor. Matilda Newport Day is celebrated annually on December 1st beginning in 1916. It was later abolished in 1980 by the military government that later overthrew the dominance of the Americo Liberian and Congolese ruling class that had ruled Liberia for a century-and-a-half.

It is unfortunate to note that I later learned in more detail about the true history of my birth country, Liberia, while serving prison time in a United States federal prison. What an odd place to learn about your country's history. Rents and lease money collected from properties occupied by the Liberian government were mostly invested overseas by the ruling class. Since almost all the property owners were working in the Liberian government, there was no incentive for the government to build buildings for the official use of the government. Being the government landlords was beneficial for the Congolese and Americo Liberian ruling class. Out of the wealth collected from Librarian taxpayers, the ruling elites were able to pay for their children's education at some of the best universities overseas and vacation in some of the best places in the USA and Europe, along with other developing African capital cities, thereby neglecting the educational systems in Liberia.

Providentially for the children of the elite ruling class, they were able to avoid being less educated in underprepared schools and universities in Liberia. The Congo's elites, after attaining some level of satisfaction and influence within the Liberian society, soon realized that the educational system, particularly the government schools, were a mess, and ill-equipped to meet the educational needs of their children, whom they were preparing to continue their legacy of domination over the native underclass. So, sending their children overseas to be educated seemed like a wise investment. The willful neglect and subjugation of the native tribes in Liberia occurred beyond the 1800s.

The disastrous, brutal treatment of the indigenous Liberians continued into the 19th century as well. In 1927, the Liberian government was accused by the League of Nations of forcibly recruiting and selling members of the indigenous tribes as contract slave workers.

A league investigation into the allegation of forced labor and slavery involving the shipment of indigenous tribes to Spanish plantations in Fernando Po, brought about the forced resignations of President Charles D.B. King and his vice president, Allen Yancy. This resulted in the subsequent election of Edwin Barclay to the presidency in 1931. In its official document, the League of Nations warned the Liberian government against "systematically fostering and encouraging a policy of gross intimidation and suppression over years to prevent citizens from asserting themselves in any way whatsoever, for the benefit of the dominant and colonizing race, though from the same African stock as themselves."(Dunn, Elwood D., et. al.)

For more than a century the free Black Americans and their descendants, who later became known as Americo Liberians, along with the rescued Congolese slaves who later ascended to the ruling upper class of Liberian society structurally denied the majority native underclass any acknowledgment of citizenship in their own homeland. This blatant and purposeful subjugation of the native majority lasted well into the start of the twentieth century, when amelioration was fostered to give all Liberian citizens the right to full participation in the nation's political process, and finally the right to vote for a person of their own choice.

After nearly a century of suppressive and subjugated rules by the free Black American settlers and their Congolese compatriots, change finally came to the native population under the "Open-Door and Unification and Integration" policy of then-president William V. S. Tubman. Tubman, who was the longest-serving president in the nation's history, initiated a policy of inclusion when he assumed office. He served from 1944 to 1971 and is considered by many the father of modern Liberia and a true friend of the native population. Even until today, many of the older generations among the native Liberian population are still mesmerized by the Tubman administration. Though the changes under him were mundane and sometimes misapplied, the older generations of Liberians, particularly the natives, recount his regime as Liberia's best days.

When I am with my family members who lived during the Tubman administration, I am often enthralled by their vivid descriptions and memories of that era. The older generation of Liberians refer to the Tubman era as the "good old days," or, "When we were, we." I am not quite sure what that means to this date. Although I was content with the experience of growing up in Liberia under the administration of Tolbert and Samuel Doe, and with my limited knowledge at the time, I thought those were the best days of Liberia. I just think it is one of the facts about life that each generation thinks that their generation was the best. However, whenever I listen to the older folks' descriptions of how life was under the Tubman administration, I warmly envy them and only wish that I could have been a part of their "good old days."

Under President Tubman's "open door" policy, Liberia experienced significant growth and prosperity that were shared not only by the ruling elite class, but by the indigenous class as well. Because Liberia was the only African country aside from Ethiopia that was not under colonial control at the time and was partially Democratic, the "open door" policy attracted increased direct foreign investments and attractions from abroad. Suddenly an influx of other Africans from the west, south, east and north of the African continent immigrated to the Liberian shore in search of freedom, liberty, and prosperity. Liberia under President Tubman served as a magnet for people escaping the ugly hand of oppression, western colonization, and brutal apartheid regime rule in South Africa. At the time, Liberia had been the only Black free land, attracting oppressed people from the Caribbean islands, Middle East, Latin America, and the West Indies as well.

Tubman's Unification and Integration policy was of particular benefit to the native majority, mostly from the interior and countryside of Liberia. His unification and integration policies focused on relocating the native population, otherwise known as the "country people," from the dark and isolated part of the country and connecting them with the coastal ruling elite class. He aimed to bring all Liberians together, irrespective of their background as one people, one nation. Before the Tubman presidency, relationships between the native population or the so-called "country people" and the coastal ruling elite class were nonexistent. There were barricades of nearly 40 miles separating the natives from the opulence and comfort of Monrovia, where the ruling elite dined and celebrated in wealth taken from the nation's resources.

Before Tubman, there was an attempt made by then-president Arthur Barclay, who was born in Barbados, to establish direct cooperation with the native tribes of Liberia and the ruling minority class made of free Black American and the Congo people. Having taken a loan from London in 1907 to carry on his policy of direct cooperation with the natives, he made meaningful efforts at reform and cooperation with the tribes. However, the London debt soon became a burden to his administration. As a result of the debt, his government was unable to exert effective authority over the interior of the countryside for more than 20 miles inland.

The burden of the London debt not only hampered the chances of the group's cooperation between the coastal elites and natives, it also forced the Liberian government to relinquish 2000, square miles of the hinterland to France in 1919 through a previous agreement. Before the agreement, the Liberian government had claim to the area, but due to the debt burden, it could no longer afford to control the territory. This effort at cooperation was the first recorded attempt made by the free Black American ruling class aimed at bringing the natives closer to them. Meanwhile, President Tubman gingerly removed the nearly 40-mile barrier separating the two groups. By removing the barricade, he was able to connect the native population from the interior and the countryside with Monrovia, where the people who ruled for more than a century resided comfortably.

In his acknowledgment of the abuse, subjugation, and oppression that the natives endured from the majority ruling class, President Tubman relayed an important message to the indigenous majority after his ascent as head of state, "As I reflect upon the condition under which you were living in 1944 when we took office, I can recall how at my first interior council, you complained of, and I discovered that district commissioners were unrestrained in their imposition of fines upon you and your people, that for the most insignificant acts your chiefs, wives, and children were humiliated and imprisoned, that you were compelled to bury your manhood and bow down to them as though they were your masters and lords instead of your public servants. I further recall that you couldn't exercise or enjoy one of your basic rights as citizens to vote for those whom you wanted to represent you, that you were not even represented in the national legislature, yet you were compelled to pay taxes like every other citizen. I still further recall that there were few roads, if any, running to or through your respective provinces, districts, towns, and villages; that you, your sons, and even your wives, sisters, and daughters were compelled to carry hammocks and loads on their heads and backs; that there were no schools; no hospitals, no medical clinics .."

In his first speech directly to the natives' majority populations, President Tubman diagnosed and shined a light on the inhumane conditions of the suffering natives which had been in existence since the founding of the Liberian nation by the free Black American slaves. The irony of Tubman's diagnosis of the plight of the Liberian indigenous population shared a broader similarity with the experience of the freed Black American slaves during their time in slavery in America. The Black American story resembles that of the native Liberian story. The only difference was that instead of being the victims of oppressive policy, they were now the perpetrators of those same policies that drove them to settle on the coastal land.

The Black American narrative begins with white Europeans escaping persecution and brutality in Europe by settling in Virginia and later in other colonies in North America. These new settlers, in their desperation to survive and amass wealth, came to terrorize, oppress and systematically kill Native American Indians, whose land they had settled on. After strong resistance from the Native Americans, the European settlers turned toward slavery as an industry and began importing Black Africans to the new colonies as slaves. Throughout slavery and up to the eventual abolition of the inhumane practice, Black Africans were denied their citizenship rights, the right to vote or to be accepted as a human being worthy of decency. Blacks were treated as an inferior class in America, the very country of their birth which came by accident. They were denied the right to education, the right to assemble freely and to seek justice in any matter of concern. Just like the native Liberians, Black Americans had no say in the government and the legislation that governed them. This brutal oppression of Black Americans went on for centuries before amelioration was made to integrate Blacks and other minority groups into the larger American society. Unfortunately, it cost the United States of America a brutal civil war to finally acknowledge the rights of all its citizens.

CHAPTER 9

THE BUILDING OF A MODERN NATION

Photo by: Alvin E. Sieh

After nearly a century-and-a-half of oppressive and subjugate rule by the Black American settlers, rescued African slaves from the Congo in Liberia saw a different shift in leadership, followed by a brand-new awakening under the stewardship of President William V.S. Tubman. When Tubman came to power, he quickly acknowledged the brutal treatment and desolate isolation of the native population from every facet of the Liberian social class. The Tubman administration enacted a series of national policies to address the economic, political and social conditions of the native majority. Famous among his policy initiatives were the "Open-Door and Unification and Integration Policy." Under this policy, Liberia saw a boost in direct foreign investment and an influx of migrants from across the continent, all in search of economic prosperity, freedom, and liberty in the small West African country of Liberia.

As Liberia accepted the U.S. dollar as its legal currency, replacing the British West African currency, it attracted more foreign investment from around the world. Under the Tubman administration of Africa's oldest republic, a significant economic boom was overseen. Liberia's capital, Monrovia, seat of the government of Liberia and the elite ruling class, benefited from a unique transformation under the "Open Door Policy." Monrovia went from being an isolated city for the ruling elites to an integrated modern city for all with few restrictions. Tubman's integration policy eradicated the nearly 40-mile boundaries that separated the Monrovia coastal ruling elites from the native majority, or "country people," and joined the different corridors of the nation, allowing the free flow of people and goods.

Tubman also oversaw the building of road networks connecting some of the country's farthest interiors to the capital city. However, between 1946 and 1960, the Tubman administration and its "Open Door" policy enjoyed extensive economic growth and development. Tubman's economic development also created real paying jobs for the native underclass, thus making it possible for some to migrate to Monrovia and other urban areas of the country. Tubman, through his outreach efforts, became a symbol and godfather for the natives who were now slowly merging into the middle class. By recognizing the uniqueness and appreciation of native culture and customs, he commended their loyalty support and admiration. Tubman demonstrated his appreciation for the indigenous culture and customs by wearing traditional Liberian-made clothing to official functions, which was rarely seen in his predecessors, all of whom stuck to Western dress codes.

As Tubman spent time raising Liberia from its dark ugly past, he also played a major role on the international stage. He worked with the United States and its allies, thereby officially entering the theater of war. After election to his first term in 1943, Liberia declared war against Germany and Japan in January of 1944.

In April, Liberia signed the Declaration of the United Nations, and in December of 1960 Liberia became a member of the UN Security Council, and from that point on Liberia took an active role in African and international affairs. Tubman made sure to uphold previous international agreements entered by his predecessors. Liberia became crucial to the United States and its allies during World War II. At the outbreak of the war, Liberia's rubber plantations were the only source of natural latex rubber available to the allies apart from a plantation in Ceylon. As an ally and America's strongest supporter on the

African continent, President Tubman was invited to Washington, DC as a guest of President Franklin Roosevelt at the White House. Tubman was the first African president to be invited as the guest of a sitting American president. He also finessed Liberia's enhanced political ties with fellow African heads of state and represented Liberia in the Asian African conference of 1955.

Meanwhile, as more and more African states were pursuing independence, he became a pioneer in the cause to liberate Africa from the iron fist of colonial rule and apartheid. Tubman further represented Liberia in Accra, Ghana for the meeting of independent African nations held in 1955 (Dunn, E, 2009). Tubman was instrumental in promoting solidarity among African nations calling for self-government and independence from colonial rule. He co-sponsored and hosted a conference of African heads of state in one of Liberia's capital cities, Sanniquellie, in Nimba County. In attendance were the PM of Ghana, Dr. Kwame Nkrumah, and Sekou Toure of the Republic of Guinea. The meeting led to the formation of African Unity OAU. In May of 1961 Liberia, under the Tubman administration, championed the creation of the Organization of African Unity. Although Liberia and Ethiopia escaped the brutal grip of colonial exploitation, they were active in the call for the elimination of apartheid and the decolonization of African nations from European colonizers.

Despite all of Tubman's accomplishments both on the domestic and international stages, some critics claimed that his administration did not do enough to develop the country. His critics point to Liberia's prosperous economic growth at the time and claimed that the development the nation underwent did not equal the economic boom sustained under Tubman's administration.

Robert Clower, in his book, *Growth Without Development,* argued this claim. Clower pointed to the disparity between the Gross National Product (GNP) and the Gross Domestic Product (GDP) and the economic development that the Tubman administration undertook. Clower and other critics believed that the ruling class and government officials embezzled funds out of the country that impeded the sustainable development of the nation during its economic boom.

Whatever position one may take regarding the Tubman era, it is, however, praiseworthy to note that his "Open-Door and Integration" policy was the catalyst for finally embracing the native majority into the mainstream of Liberian society. It is worth noting that it took the free Black American founders of the nation nearly a century-and-a-half without acknowledging the citizenship of the indigenous Liberian majority. It took Tubman less than two years to acknowledge the inhumane treatment of those same people. Upon recognizing their plight, he vociferously began the process of unification and integration of the interior and the countryside of the coastal areas of Monrovia. Tubman ensured that the interior people had a voice in the affairs of government that ruled over their lives by enabling them to cast their own votes.

Reflecting on the accomplishments of William V.S. Tubman through unprejudiced eyes, it is only fair to give this son of Africa his due, not only as a godfather of Liberia but also as one of the godfathers of Africa and a permanent figure in the arena of history worthy of being studied.

It is time for Liberians and Africans everywhere to begin learning about their heritage and history. Instead of the history of those who suppressed and subjugated them as inferior beings, they are worthy of being lionized. While there is nothing wrong with learning about the histories of other people, published narratives may not be accurate, because sometimes history comes from a prejudiced or predisposed viewpoint.

CHAPTER 10

THE LIFE AND DEATH OF PRESIDENT WILLIAM R. TOLBERT

After the untimely death of the father of modern Liberia, William V.S Tubman, in 1971 at a clinic in London, the affairs of state were transferred to his Vice President, William Richard Tolbert Jr. Before ascending to the presidency not much was known of the newly appointed vice president, who took over a country that was mourning over the loss of its beloved and longest-serving president.

Not much was known about the new president because he served in the shadow of the late President Tubman. After nearly 19 years of service not much was known about Tolbert's policy agendas, both domestic and international. There was intense curiosity regarding the policy agendas he would pursue. Liberian allies, particularly the United States of America, were in imminent need of the new Liberian government's support, especially at a time when communism ideologies were spreading around the African continent at an alarming rate.

When Tolbert took over as head of state of Liberia, a decline in world prices for its major exports, iron ore and natural rubber, was putting a budget strain on the government's ability to meet policy agendas. As a result, the Liberian economy was experiencing financial hardships during the early part of the 1970s. To remedy the problem, the government took on foreign loans to help sustain the economy.

Tolbert was presiding over a nation where the Americo Liberian and the Congo elite classes represented about 15 percent of the population. However, they had overwhelming control of Liberia's political and economic arenas. The new president also had other challenges on his hands regarding the condition and concerns of the native majority who, until Tubman's presidency, had been excluded from the nation's economic and political prosperity.

Before Tubman, native participation in the Liberian government was mostly paying taxes and fines to a government that never acknowledged their existence as citizens of a land that they belonged to. Their representation as citizens of Liberia was excluded from national funding documents for nearly a century-and-a-half. However, when the native majority was finally acknowledged by the late Tubman administration, it was forced to abide by laws written in the language of the Black American settlers. It was in a language they did not understand, read or write. Although the native majorities were pleased to be integrated into the mainstream of Liberia modern society, they were not prepared to deal with the challenges to come.

Before Tubman, Liberia was a divided country. The native majority was isolated in the interior of the country, while the ruling elite consisted of Americo Liberians and the Congo elite occupying the affluent coastal areas of the country. To his credit, Tubman made a concerted effort in unifying the two sides. However, his administration failed to enact an educational system that would have helped the disconnected natives make a living, which is the first essential element in any modern society.

Before the arrival of the free Black Americans, the natives had always benefited from the wealth of the coastal territories that they occupied; they knew how to grow food abundantly. Rather than teaching and empowering the indigenous to employ scientific methods in cultivating their land and fields, they were removed from some of these places they had come to depend on before the freed settlers' arrival in the 1800s. Isolated from farming on their lands, they now possessed skills that did not benefit them. Schools built by the Liberian government in the provinces and districts did nothing to make the natives productive at creating a thriving economy with the ability to participate in modern commerce.

Meanwhile, as concern built up around the new president's policy agendas, Tolbert surprised everyone with his independent thinking. The truth is Tolbert was unrestrained by the Tubman government's appeasement policy. He was an independent freethinker and a man with a mind of his own. As he began to implement his own independent and unapologetic views, he soon found himself with opposing views from those of one of its primary supporters, the United States of America. As he began to establish himself, he quickly moved away from his predecessor's appeasement policies with America and began fostering new allies in places deemed hostile to U.S. interests and policies.

Tolbert also opposed his predecessor's foreign policy and world views. Tubman objected to any form of communism. He sided with the United States on everything anti-communist. Tubman stood side by side with the United States, voting on all occasions along with all U.S. allies and supporting the U.S. war effort in Vietnam. Meanwhile, Tolbert had a different view regarding U.S.-Liberia relationships. He was of the view that a scrounger crying out for help should not care where his handout came from so long as that handout lifted him from his destitute condition.

Tolbert immediately revisited all Liberia concession agreements that were heavily beneficial to foreign investors. At the time, most of Liberia's concession agreements granted foreign companies large tax incentives and privileges without asking for any meaningful investment so long as it benefited the corrupt bank accounts and pockets of those signing the agreements. Most of the country's concession agreements offered nothing for the poor suffering masses. For example, some of the foreign companies that benefited from misdirected tax privileges were the multi-billion dollar Firestone Rubber company, West Germany-controlled Bong Mining Company, the (American) Republic Steel-owned Liberian Mining Company (LMC) and the Swedish dominated Mining Company (LAMCO). All these companies played a crucial role in the allied war efforts along with the reconstruction effort in America and Europe after both World Wars.

Simply put, Liberia's natural resources helped build modern America and modern Europe during Franklin Roosevelt's New Deal initiatives. Liberia was blessed with a tropical climate and natural resources. It was well-positioned to supply America and her allies with rubber latex and iron ore. With Japan's military control of Malaysia and Singapore at the time, Liberia remained the only country on earth during that time to give America and Europe what was most needed for its war effort and reconstruction endeavors.

In the 1920s, Firestone Tire and Rubber Company obtained a concession of 1,000,000 acres (400,000 hectares) for a rubber plantation outside of Monrovia for pennies on the dollar. Meanwhile, a loan was arranged through the Finance Corporation of America, a Firestone subsidiary. With this private loan, the Liberian government was able to consolidate all its external and internal debts and place the country's financial house on relatively stable footing. However, when Liberia was accused of forced labor and slavery, the allegation forced the resignation of President King and his vice president Allen Yancy. As a result of this debacle, the Liberian government started to fall into financial trouble, so it appealed to the Council of the League of Nations for financial assistance. A commission of inquiry was established to investigate the request.

Unfortunately for the government of Liberia, its loan request was met by unsuccessful attempts to work out a framework of assistance involving the appointment of foreign administrators.

The Liberian government's request for assistance from the United States and the U.K. lasted for nearly three years without fruitful outcome. Frustrated by the delays, a declaration of moratorium on the Firestone loan, and abrupt suspension of diplomatic relations with the United States and Great Britain was the response from the Liberian government. After the Council of Leagues finally withdrew its plan of assistance, the Liberian government reached a dubious agreement with Firestone for 99 years and one million acres of land at six cents an acre. This dubious contract gave Firestone the right to own any minerals discovered. Liberia was blessed with gold and diamonds, so no one knows how much gold, diamonds and other minerals were discovered by Firestone as a result of this deal. The Liberian government did not mandate Firestone to build a necessary pre-processing facility that would have created fair paying jobs and skills for the hard-working indigenous people that were working under deplorable conditions.

Regrettably, out of all of Liberia's concession agreements, only the Librarian's minority ruling class and the companies benefited from the wealth generated from these lucrative contracts. For the indigenous, they were forced to work in degrading conditions. Workers and their families lived in mud huts covered with palm leaves for roofs. There were no indoor toilets, electricity or indoor drinking water for the workers and their families. Workers laboring on the one-million-acre plantation had no uniforms or protective gears to shield them from the oppressive humidity of the Liberian dry season's heat.

Most of the workers at the multi-billion-dollar Firestone rubber plantation walked the fields barefoot, because most could not afford to buy work shoes from the money they were paid by the company. Some of the workers interviewed for this project disclosed that some of their colleagues died of snake bites and infections from injuries sustained after walking the long acres of plantation land. They also complained of getting sick with pneumonia during the uncompromising torrential rain season. The indigenous workers had no real school built for them by Firestone to educate their children. And if there had been any, they were below any means by which a human being could gain satisfactory or basic education.

On the other hand, LAMCO and Bong Mining companies had more decent housing facilities for its middle-class workers, whose job it was to control and

SLAVERY AND BLACK AMERICAN

help suppress the mostly illiterate indigenous workers from seeking anything meaningful. Both companies' housing facilities were decent in terms of Liberian standards, but inferior by European standards. None of those companies would have been allowed to build such facilities for their workers in their respective countries. Additionally, LAMCO and Bong Mining Company built schools for their workers' children to attend.

However, most of those schools were limited in their effectiveness. They were not intended to educate and train the local workers or their children with the skills needed to one day run or operate company operations or functions. Rather, they taught useless information about western greatness, conquests and subject matters that had no significance to the development of the workers' children. Instead of educating the workers and their children with the skills to create and develop the raw iron ore or rubber latex into products that the Liberian nation and the African continent could benefit from, they were taught to upload the raw materials on ships and trains to be shipped to America. In America, they were turned into useable commodities and shipped back to Liberia and the rest of the African continent to sell back to the people.

Firestone, LAMCO and Bong Mining Company all became multibillion-dollar institutions from the exploited sweat, blood and hard labor of the indigenous Liberian masses. While these companies can proudly claim that the system of capitalism benefited their investors and their western workers, the same cannot be said about the poor indigenous Liberian workers. The only things that these poor Liberian workers can claim is compounded poverty, abject illiteracy and all sorts of health-related illness from years of working in unprotected facilities owned by western multinational corporations.

Behind this backdrop the Tolbert administration renegotiated most of the Liberian concession agreements that privileged large foreign companies. It is also significant to mention that although Tolbert's foreign policy was compared with that of Tubman, his domestic policy was a total embrace of the Tubman domestic policy. Following in the footsteps of his predecessor, Tolbert enacted a bold step policy agenda that was known as the "Total Involvement for Higher Height." This policy aimed at targeting mostly the native majority population of Liberia. Another part of his bold policy, also known as the "Rally Time," was laser focused on uplifting and improving the social, economic, and educational conditions of the entire Liberian population from "mats to mattresses" or from rag to riches in the western sense.

Tolbert was of the strong conviction that a wholesome functioning society must be able to improve the livelihood of all its citizens regardless of class, religion, region or educational status. His administration zeroed in on eliminating disease, illiteracy, ignorance, tribalism and poverty as the path forward toward achieving a wholesome functioning society. Tolbert, though born to Americo Liberian parents, acquired his ideology and his concern for the plight of the indigenous people. His philosophy was a stark departure from some of his predecessors whose policies of appeasement to the United States and the isolation of the native majority were the norms.

Those who knew him best believed that as an ordained Baptist preacher Tolbert was driven or inspired by his Biblical teachings and religious views that emphasized treating everyone the same and caring for the most vulnerable in society. Inspired by his progressive beliefs, he failed to realize, or worse, refused to accept that in the arena of world politics, not everyone gets invited to political dinners, and especially not when the Cold War was at its height. Tolbert's policy of embracing and welcoming everyone soon lead him to join the Non-Aligned Movement, which at the time was comprised of nations that had independent foreign policies that were not dictated by the influence of western or eastern nations. In keeping with his policy of embracing and welcoming nations that showed signs of friendliness toward Liberia, Tolbert soon accepted economic aid from the USSR in 1974. He also accepted educational aid from the Soviet Union, Romania, Cuba, and other communist and socialist states otherwise known at the time as the Eastern Bloc.

As a result of the educational aid, several Liberian students traveled overseas to study in the respective countries that provided aid to their government. All of Tolbert's diplomatic maneuvering and outreach were happening during the height of the Cold War between the East and West at the time they were fighting each other for global dominance and influence. Meanwhile, Tolbert's policy of openness and appeasement to all nations regardless of ideological differences was not sitting well with the United States government. Tolbert in furtherance of his Non-Aligned foreign policy, accepted diplomatic relationships with some of America's strongest enemies such as the Soviet Union, Cuba, and China, among others.

Tolbert also went against the U.S. administration at the UN General Assembly and voted against Israel's treatment of the Palestinian people. In the wave of tension between East and West, it was anathema to the United States government for the Tolbert administration to pursue such a foreign policy agenda. The U.S. government had too much strategic investment in Liberia at the time to sit back idly and wait for the Soviets, Chinese, Romanians, and Cubans to come and play in her footprints on the African continent. In the height of the Cold War, Liberia was strategically positioned and suited as the ideal place for the U.S. and the West as a launch site for the fight against the total elimination of communist and socialist ideas, which were on the rise mostly in Eastern and Northern Africa.

Under Tolbert's predecessors in 1942, Liberia signed a defense agreement with the United States. This agreement resulted in the undertaking of a program of strategic road building and the construction of the Robert International Airport RIA along with a Deepwater harbor called the Freeport of Monrovia. At the same time, United States currency was declared in 1943 as the legal currency of Liberia. This agreement also led to the construction of the Voice of America (VOA), a facility that secretly handled U.S. intelligence and Foreign Service communication on the continent and around the world. The VOA also broadcast American foreign policy propaganda throughout Africa during the Cold War era and beyond.

The United States had other investments in Liberia that were worth protecting from Tolbert's communist friends, which included the OMEGA Navigation Station, which monitored communications on the African continent. The agreement also allowed the United States government to build other facilities in Liberia totally rent-free, thus taking meaningful resources from the Liberian people. At the time, Liberia was the only country on the continent hosting the largest U.S. foreign and diplomatic facilities. The United States also had private American business investments in Liberia to protect it from the communist influence, including a Coca-Cola factory, Firestone Natural Rubber plantation and LAMCO Mining Company, among others. In addition to the concerns from the United States, Tolbert was also facing growing opposition at home for his domestic policy agendas.

While there is no denying that the Tolbert policy agendas were bold and badly needed at the time when Liberia was struggling economically, it did not bear fruit fast enough to ease those who despaired of the growing underclass majority who were barely living on scraps handed down from the corrupt hands of Tolbert government officials. With all this growing tension fermenting the anger of the poor and desperate masses, Tolbert soon found himself facing his first domestic uprising when the price of a bag of rice, which is a Liberian staple, rose. The increase in the price of rice, along with growing and unrestrained rampant corruption, unemployment, nepotism, and the slow pace of improvement in ordinary Liberian lives, poised the country for violence.

In 1979, frustrated by the rising price of rice, the mostly ignored underclass majority took to the streets to demand the removal of Tolbert from office and a decrease in the price of rice. Many businesses in Monrovia were looted and several of the Tolbert government official and private homes were destroyed by angry mobs. When the riot came to an end, more than 30 people had lost their lives. To control the rioting, Tolbert turned to his friend, the late Guinean President Ahmed Sekou Toure for help. President Toure responded by dispatching his Guinean special forces, none of whom spoke English. These special forces from neighboring Guinea responded by beating and whipping demonstrators with objects such as whips, belts, cable and electrical wires of all kinds.

With pressure mounting from the angry, hopeless and frustrated citizenry, along with opposition from within the administration regarding his foreign policy agendas which were also fueled by American resentment, and growing concerns about the administration's coziness with the communists, Tolbert was now sitting on a time bomb waiting to explode. Meanwhile, several months after the rice riot, the end finally came for Tolbert. His fate has been sealed by what most observers believe was the United States government. As a Baptist preacher and a man of faith, not even his religious faith could have protected him from the hands of the 12 assassins sent to murder him.

On a dark silent night in the wee hours of April 12, 1980, when the strong sea current of the Atlantic ocean sent strong waves to the seashore behind the executive mansion where the president was asleep and Monrovians, along with the rest of the country were in deep slumber, a group of 12 enlisted assassins from the Armed Forces of Liberia, led by 28-year-old master sergeant Samuel Kenyon Doe stormed the mansion, the most heavily guarded edifice in the entire country. The assassins made their way forward, killing some of the special security forces guarding the president. They then made their way into the president's bedroom and disemboweled him, accosting him while he slept.

After killing the president in the most prestigious and highly guarded building in Liberia, the group of assassins immediately proceeded to round up all the Tolbert government and cabinet officials. More than dozens of them were arrested and imprisoned at the Barclay Training Center and the South Beach prison by the new military junta. Some Tolbert government officials managed to escape and flee into hiding.

Others were not so lucky. Foreign Minister Hon. Cecil Dennis escaped and headed toward the United States Embassy near Monrovia. Upon his arrival, he begged for asylum but was ultimately rejected by embassy officials. Minister Dennis left with nowhere to hide and was later surrendered by the new military junta forces. The minister, along with 12 other officials of the administration were publicly placed before a firing squad at the Barclay Training Center (BTC) beach and publicly executed. That dreadful day of April 12, 1980 marked a turning point in the history of Liberia. The executed men were the last standing officials of the freed Black Americans, Americo Liberian and the Congolese ruling elite class that had dominated the country's power structure for nearly a century-and-a-half. Absent any outrage from the United States government about the political carnage and bloodshed by the new military government, the United States swiftly moved to acknowledge the new military regime as the legitimate government of Liberia.

The Reagan administration began without delay to support the new military regime with U.S. taxpayer dollars, without human rights requirements. For U.S. foreign policy experts, Liberia was an important partner to the U.S. role in defeating communism, and Tolbert was viewed as an unwilling partner in that effort. For Americans, Tolbert was an obstacle and a consequential threat to American foreign policy agendas, and the Doe regime seemed appropriate for their foreign policy pursuit. According to inside observers, the U.S. CIA footprint was visible everywhere leading to the assassination of the late Liberian President William R. Tolbert. Many observers believe that the men who led the coup did not have the acumen or the training to carry out such an elaborate coup without the design and support of the CIA or the Reagan Administration. This is an allegation that is difficult to prove; however, looking at politics and U.S. foreign policy concerns at the time, one can understand why the U.S. government would want to see Tolbert disappear from the scene.

CHAPTER 11

SAMUEL KENYON DOE FAILS FELLOW LIBERIAN NATIVES

Photo by: Alvin L. Sieh

After the assassination of President William R. Tolbert Jr, on April 12, 1980, the new military government known as the People's Redemption Council (PRC) was viewed by the majority indigenous group that had been isolated from the nation's wealth and politics for over 100 years as the answer to their prayers for an inclusive country. To its credit, the Reagan administration also held the view that the new military council members and the new heads of state, all of whom came from the majority indigenous tribes of Liberia, would eventually open the door toward a fair democratic system of government in Liberia.

Samuel Doe came to power in Liberia at the height of the Cold War between East and West. America's investments in Liberia were a geopolitical asset in the fight against the spread of communism in Africa and the Middle East. Tolbert was considered by the Americans as an impediment toward their cause when he invited some of America's enemies to play on the American playground. In the eyes of America, he and his government were expendable. President Samuel Doe, the new head of state of the Liberian government, became an astute and particularly important ally to the American government.

The Reagan administration, with its overflow of U.S. dollars, kept the new military regime of Samuel Doe afloat, pumping millions of U.S. dollars in financial and military aid into Liberia. It is estimated that within six years the Doe government received about five hundred million dollars in financial assistance from the administration. Meanwhile, the relationship between the two countries was at its best. The Doe administration pledged its commitment to the protection and preservation of the longstanding historical relationships between Liberia and the United States. The Doe government also granted access for Americans to use Liberia's air space, along with its port for U.S. troop deployment when needed.

However, before the new Liberian military government was considered as the legitimate government by African nations, it was Libyan leader Muammar Gaddafi who first legitimized the Doe administration. Gaddafi also extended his financial and military promise to support the new military government. The Libyan leader promised to build a Libyan people's bureau in Monrovia followed by other Libyan investments in housing and other areas of interest. Meanwhile, the Libyan leader's hand of goodwill extension did not sit well with the Reagan Administration or the U.S. government.

Furthermore, the Reagan administration pressured the Doe administration to dichotomize ties with the Libyan government. Under pressure from the U.S. government, the Doe regime closed the Libyan mission in Liberia and rejected Gaddafi's financial support and military assistance. Doe also took further steps by cutting down the number of Soviet Union embassy and diplomatic staff. In addition, the Communist Chinese diplomatic staff was also kept at skeletal levels at the request of the U.S. government.

Relations between the late Tolbert government and the state of Israel had been strained. Under the Doe administration, the relationship was reestablished and in return, the Israeli government trained the Liberian Special Anti-Terrorist Unit known as "SATU." The special unit provided extra layers of security for President Doe and his government officials. While the administration was enjoying U.S. government support, it was also carrying on political persecution and human rights abuses against opposition or former members of the PRC who defected or were against the idea of the perpetuity of military rule.

Unfortunately for the opposition and the people of Liberia, the Reagan administration kept a non- interference policy and ignored opposition cries during the initial stage of the abuse of power. At the time, the Doe administration was among the regimes placed on the U.S. government's special security, program making it one of the highest recipients of U.S. special security assistance aid. At the time, the Doe administration received more U.S. taxpayer dollars than any other country in sub-Saharan Africa. Despite Doe's lack of bold vision for Liberia, coupled with his human rights abuses at home, the Reagan administration steadfastly maintained its support for the regime and kept it afloat in spite of concerns from Liberian political corners, along with other international organizations that were raising concerns about abuses of power. For the U.S. government, whatever it took to keep the Libyan, Soviet and Chinese influences out of the American playground Liberia, the Reagan administration went to great lengths to foster without restraining the Doe government's abuse of power.

In return, Doe did for the Americans whatever they asked of him, so it was wise for the Americans to turn a blind eye as Doe continued to violate American core values so long it was kept away from the American public eye. With the influx of U.S. dollars pulling into the Liberian government coffers, the Doe administration had no bold policy agenda to benefit the Liberian people. Doe, unlike his predecessors Tolbert and Tubman, both of whom had policy agendas, had no fixed policy agenda.

Tubman was known for building a modern city and making Liberia well-known on the international stage and supporting newly liberated African nations emerging from the rigid hands of western imperialism and colonial control. Tolbert also had a bold policy agenda: at the height of the cold war and during the acrimonious struggle between East and West, he decided to not follow the path of his predecessor by appeasing the U.S. government's foreign policy pursuits. On the international front, he cultivated friends and extended a hand to countries that were considered aggressive toward U.S. foreign policy goals.

Tolbert wanted to be fair and balanced in his foreign policy pursuits. He believed that Liberia should be able and free to align with any country of its choice without interference from outside forces. On the domestic front, his agenda of "total involvement and higher heights" was geared toward uplifting the indigenous majority and underclass from poverty and into the mainstream of Liberian middle-class society. He was of the belief that a "wholesome functioning society can only prosper by the total involvement of all of its citizenry." Though both presidents' policies had their flaws, one cannot argue that they both failed to have bold agendas for the Liberian people.

After the assassination of President Tolbert, Samuel K. Doe, a master sergeant, was believed to be the first indigenous African Liberian son of the land. Unlike all his predecessors, Doe did not have an American heritage or ancestry connection to the freed Black Americans who founded the small nation of Liberia. He came from one of Liberia's indigenous tribes called "Kran." The Kran tribes are from the northern region of Liberia close to the Ivorian border. Both his parents were indigenous African Liberians.

Doe's parents, like most indigenous Liberian parents at the time, were born and raised in a nation ruled by former slaves from America and their descendants. They were born in a nation where they could not write, read or understand the official language in which the laws or constitution were written. They lived in a nation where they were not privileged or allowed to learn or participate in the system of government that they were governed by. Out of this deprived background emerged a man born into disadvantaged conditions, and he ascended to the presidency of a nation that kept him and millions more like him away from the corridors of opportunity. For many, or perhaps for the entire native majority population, Samuel K. Doe was an angel sent from above to ameliorate the wrong done to them by the minority elite class of Black American hegemony over their lives.

With just an elementary school education, (although some reports say a junior high school education), he rose above his early circumstances. Doe took seriously his role as head of state of Africa's oldest independent nation founded by freed black slaves from America in search of a free colony to call home that was far away from the brutal hands of slavery and brutality by white slave owners, and a system of government that perpetuated its existence. Although there was resistance to settlement in the new Liberian colony, they prevailed in establishing a Black-owned independent nation free of white rule or hegemony.

As Liberia became a nation, the settlers' view of a nation meant the isolation of the native majority indigenous population. In the formation of the nation's founding documents, they willfully ostracized the indigenous Liberian people that they met on their arrival in their new land. The free Black American settlers kept citizenship rights only for themselves. They viewed the indigenous African Liberian tribes as inferior and uncivilized to mingle with, a belief system indoctrinated in them by their former white slave masters in America.

The African slaves brought to America were made to renounce their religion, culture, customs, names and family ties. Their identities were confiscated and thrown away in the graveyards of ignorance. Blacks held in bondage in America and across Europe were made to believe that the gods of Western civilizations strongly decried their skin colors or Blackness, culture, customs, way of life and worst of all, their mere existence as a species of the human race. The slave masters and the planters of western civilization bore into the minds of these vulnerable enslaved Black Africans that the color black was a distasteful thing to associate with. Some of these ignorant white slaveholders at the time considered a person of black skin as an animal of certain lower status that must be inferior to the white race. These notions about people of color were widely spread in England amongst the racist white race of England. Before 1600 the English Oxford Dictionary described the color black as "deeply stained with dirt; soiled, dirty, foul, having, dark or deadly purpose, involving death, deadly; baneful, disastrous, sinister, iniquitous, atrocious, terribly wicked, indicating disgrace, censure, liability to punishment, etc."

These extremely insulting and shameful descriptions of the color black were maliciously crafted by racist white men to belittle the Black race. By these descriptions slave masters and some racist members of the white race used these shameful terms augment their ill-treatment of the Blacks amongst them, including those held as slaves. By these depictions, racist whites were able to dehumanize people of black color by referring to them as animal-like. Unfortunately for the Black race, their white handlers over time were able to miseducate some of them into believing that their color and race were inferior to that of the so-called white race. The effect of their propaganda has had a lasting effect on the psyches of both Blacks and whites. Sadly, for some amongst the Black race, they have been bamboozled into looking down upon their own kind and sometimes comparing them to savages or an uncivilized bunch of ingrates. Depending on the geographical location of certain Blacks, they might be inclined to suggest to Blacks from different geographical locations as inferior and prone to claim supremacy over them because of skin tone or unique coloration. Rather than acknowledging that though we might be different culturally and in skin tone, which is just the uniqueness of our Black race, these ignorant Blacks persist in unwittingly claiming to be superior to Blacks of certain skin tones and locations. This is a trick from the playbook of racist white masters that has been burnt into the consciousness of some Blacks, especially those living in the west.

Meanwhile, the freed Black settlers in Liberia were of the distorted mindset that they were superior to the indigenous African Liberians whom they met on their native land. The settlers not only looked down on the blackness of the natives, they also looked down on their culture, customs, art, literature, history and the very way of life of the diverse indigenous African Liberian tribes. Rather than invite the diversity and the unique cultural richness of the indigenous people and build a more prosperous and vibrant nation for the two groups, the settlers deliberately ostracized them from the affairs of building a new nation to which they all had legitimate claims.

With this backdrop, the ascension of Samuel Doe as head of state was applauded and received as a gift for the indigenous majority population of Liberia, who had suffered under the brutal and corrupt hands of the minority elite ruling class of Americo Liberians and their Congolese cronies. Unfortunately for the indigenous Liberians, Samuel Doe turned out to be a disappointing failure to the native majority. Doe did not have a bold vision to uplift the suffering indigenous majority population from abject poverty, illiteracy and the culture of laziness. Doe created divisions among the various tribes. He accelerated corruption, nepotism, and tribalism to a level unseen by many in the nation's history.

Rather than breaking down the systems and barriers that had held down the native underclass majority from moving forward, he created division and conflict among the tribes. Doe continued to unleash his brutal reign on the people of Liberia without being punished by the Americans who rained down U.S. taxpayer dollars on him. Reagan's administration only stepped in when the Cold War was waning, and America's Cold War enemies no longer posed a significant strategic threat to its foreign policy interests. Therefore, it was no longer in the foreign policy interest of the Reagan administration to continue keeping the Doe administration afloat, especially in the mix of all the human rights abuses that had been reported about the regime.

When Doe's U.S. dollar supplies ran stagnant, he printed Liberian currency through a British company. The Liberian currency that was once tied closely to the U.S. dollar quickly turned into the equivalent of Monopoly money. With no resources and tangible monetary policy in place to back the new Liberian currency, the Liberian dollar became unreliable and worthless. There was growing criticism and pressure from both home and abroad to turn the country over to civilian rule. In response, it was Doe's idea of grand apostasy to announce his resignation as commander in chief of the Armed Forces of

Liberia, and he hastened to declare himself a civilian. He decided to campaign as a candidate for the presidency, representing the National Democratic Party of Liberia (NDPL). There was nothing democratic about the NDPL; the party was filled mostly with Doe's tribesmen and loyalists. Although Doe claimed to have resigned from the armed services, he was technically the commander in chief of the AFL, and he maintained firm control over all the institutions that ran the election commission. He ensured the security apparatuses that made sure that voters and even opposition political leaders were safe and free to exercise their constitutional rights. He also had formal control over the judiciary which was filled with his appointees and cronies. Critics from the opposition parties and the progressive student union from the University of Liberia raised alarms about the uneven field in the political process that was taking shape and became nervous, crying foul. Students from the University of Liberia responded by staging peaceful demonstrations demanding that President Samuel Doe not participate in the upcoming Liberian election.

Meanwhile, Doe responded by accusing the opposition parties of inciting violence and undermining his administration. Paranoid by the opposition against him, Doe responded by rounding up and imprisoning his political opponents. Some of the student leaders leading the demonstration against him were also imprisoned by his security forces. On the campus of the University of Liberia, there were reports of female students being raped by the president's security forces and soldiers that were brought from nearby barracks to quell the demonstration.

Despite the outcries of opposition leaders, Doe managed to manipulate the election and eventually won overwhelmingly by racking the vote. As president, Doe tightened his grip on progressive opposition party leaders. Many of his opposition party leaders went into exile to protect themselves from his brutal regime. However, one of the compatriots was not so lucky when he attempted to overthrow Doe by entering Liberia from the neighboring country of Sierra Leone. The leader of the botched attempted coup was Doe's former commanding general, Thomas Quwonpa, who was among the military assassins that stormed the executive mansion on April 12 of 1980 to overthrow then sitting President William R. Tolbert.

General Quwonpa was respected among the PRC members. According to inside sources and in his statement, he stated that he fell off with the Doe government because Doe wanted to seize power after the overthrow of Tolbert's administration. In his announcement after declaring his brief takeover of the Liberian Broadcasting Station, he stated that he had no interest in becoming head of state. "I came to remove Doe and turn the country back to the Liberian people so that they can have a free and fair election." However, after his botched attempted coup against his former boss, Samuel Doe, who eventually emerged from his hidden place, unleashed his men in the corridors of Monrovia. Soon Quwonpa and his men were hunted down in every corner of Monrovia by Doe's special security force and the first infantry battalion troops from Camp Scheifling stationed outside of Monrovia. In less than 24 hours, Quwonpa, along with other members of the military and civilians who were believed to be his supporters were apprehended many were killed and the lucky ones were imprisoned.

Unfortunately for some of the ordinary Liberians rejoicing upon hearing the news of Doe's being overthrown, also experienced the unfriendly and ruthless hands of Doe's men. There were also rumors of Doe being captured by Quwonpa and his men during the upheaval the morning of the botched coup attempt. According to spoken accounts, Doe promised the men holding him a huge sum of money and high positions in his government if they let him go free. However true the information might be, Doe was able to return as head of state and as a wounded lion. He responded by unleashing his henchmen, made mostly of his fellow tribe men into Nimba County and other localities where members of the Gio and Mano tribes resided.

General Quwonpa and members of his rebellion team were mostly from the Gio and Mano tribes. Many members of his tribes were murdered by Doe's henchmen. Quwonpa himself was eventually captured and killed. His body was chopped into pieces and paraded around the capital city of Monrovia for all to see.

The news of the botched coup was difficult for many Liberian to accept, as it was a disappointment for many who were looking forward to the end of the Doe regime. For Doe's supporters, they were extremely excited that their hero survived the botched coup attempt. There were also rumors of how Doe used African science or voodoo to disappear from the midst of his captives by impairing them.

After the death of Quwonpa, Doe and his bloodthirsty security forces unleashed a retaliatory campaign against the members of the Gio and Mano tribes, killing them at will. The retaliatory raid and indiscriminate killing by mostly Krahn soldiers from President Doe's ethnic group would set the stage for prolonged civil wars in Liberia.

By 1989, there was a full civil war in Liberia that was waged very much along tribal lines. The war finally dealt a big enough blow dash the indigenous majority hopes of a unified nation. It would require international help to bring peace back to Liberia and restore hope for a promising democracy again. When Doe was presented on the world stage as the first-ever indigenous president, the Liberian people and the world expected him to embark on a transformational change in every sector of the Liberian society. He was presented with a unique opportunity to unify the country by eradicating centuries-old barriers that had held down the native majority from participating in the democratic process in their homeland. Doe had the chance to finally eradicate illiteracy, poverty, disease and abject ignorance that has kept the native majority population in poverty and submission to the Americo-Liberian and the Congolese ruling class.

Unlike his predecessor, Doe did not usher in a bold plan to repair the fundamental decay in Liberian society. Rather, Doe squandered the opportunity to empower the native majority with an educational system that addressed their plight. As the first real indigenous president, it was expected that Doe would draw attention to building an educational system for the natives that was not based on useless memorization of the history of the West and America. The indigenous people wanted no more false narratives about the life of Christopher Columbus, Shakespeare, or Alexander the Great while looking down on Liberia's heroes and its cultural significance and contributions to the world. The time was right for Doe to implement a bold policy agenda that was geared toward building an educational system based not on endless memorization of political-economic or social policy pulled right out of colonial or imperialist playbooks or ideology that had no significant or applicable foothold in addressing the real educational needs of the native majority.

I am not advocating for an educational system that eliminates proven concepts. If a Western discovery proves to be significant to the empowerment and economic or social enrichment of the African people, there is no doubt that they should pursue the knowledge for its advancement. What good is it for an indigenous African to earn a degree in social science or literature that is designed by Western educators and meant to address the social or literary issues in Western society? He or she may not be able to properly apply the degree or its concepts in a remote village or town in Africa. If one demands its application in a remote village or town in Africa, the student or professional would be miseducating the population because the two cultures differ widely, and the social economic and political climates do not provide the opportunity for such implementation. Liberia and many other African countries find themselves inheriting educational systems designed by Western educators with a Western diagnostic of Africans, and African societies and cultures. They pretend to find the cure for Africa's problems by encouraging African society to adopt Western solutions to African problems.

Unfortunately, many miseducated African leaders continue to believe in these diabolical concepts and then wonder why their country fails to move forward. Imperialist colonial rulers have left the African continent; however, the grassroots and system that brought it to life remains within African society, perpetrated by past and present miseducated leaders. If anyone doubts this, just look around Africa and examine its political, economic, educational systems, social justice issues, etc. They all fail to meet the needs of the struggling masses. The so-called Western systems designed to help the people of Africa will dishearten its progressive-minded populations.

All the abysmal institutions in Africa which are following Western or colonial blueprints and methods are misinformed. The question that needs to be asked for those who believe that Western systems are adaptable in Africa is why all of these institutions in Africa are run by mostly Western-educated Africans who fail to measure up to addressing the needs of the people they were designed to help?

There is no denying that it took Liberia more than a century-and-a-half to arrive at where it was under the Doe administration. Therefore, it is only fair to acknowledge that nearly a decade under Doe did not lift Liberia out of its century-old decay. Because Samuel Doe had limited education equivalent to that of an elementary or junior high school student, the affairs of governing and their intricate social, economic and geopolitical structure was too enormous and complex for him to comprehend. Unfortunately for the marginally educated head of state, those around him masquerading as educated men and women were themselves miseducated by a system that was earlier designed to keep them inferior to the Americo- Liberian and their Congo cronies. To his credit, realizing the need for education, despite his lack of knowledge that the educational system in Liberia was designed to miseducate him, he gallantly struggled to acquire an education while serving as head of state.

Doe's perseverance must be commended for a man who couldn't speak standard Liberian English when he first took over as head of state to address the united nation and the American people during a state visit at the White

House as an official guest of President Reagan. However, because Doe was educated in a failed educational system designed to manipulate him as a puppet of the West and inferior to their demands, he was unable to further any meaningful policy agenda that would lift the indigenous Liberians out of their servitude from the Western system that was imposed on them by the freed Black American settlers. As a result of these missed opportunities and incorrect guidance, Samuel Doe could never seize the moment to turn Liberia into an economic magnet in Africa, or at least in West Africa.

Liberia with all its rain forests offered an endless amount of tropical fruits, rivers, and widespread oceanfront beaches, but it could not boast of having an industry that supplied the rest of the continent with its tropical fruits or vegetables. Rich with gold, diamonds, rubber, iron ore, timber, and so many tropical crops that were in world demand, it didn't have a processing factory of its own for these commodities to succeed on the world market with the label, "Made in Liberia." Blessed with lakes, blue ocean views and mountains, it could not boast of being a tourism destination in Africa. Liberia has one of the oldest constitutions in modern world democracy. It also has the first Black-owned modern system of government in the world.

Additionally, Black Americans share a lot of historical ties with Liberia that date back to 1816, yet extraordinarily little social, economic, political, cultural and educational exchange takes place between the two groups. Most Black Americans would prefer traveling to Jamaica, Mexico, Europe and the Caribbean for vacation rather than travel to Liberia, a country that was founded by their ancestors in Africa. In fact, most Black Americans are more knowledgeable about the history, social lives, political, economics and culture of Jamaica, Mexico, Europe and the Caribbean than about Liberia, the country that their forefathers bled, sweat and died to found. I am not arguing that it was Samuel Doe's fault for not cultivating the relationships; it was also the fault of Black Americans in the U.S. for not embracing their African roots. Liberia, Jamaica, and the Caribbean's Islands have similar climate and tropical coastlines, and if Liberia was given the attention by Black Americans that it deserves, it could be transformed into a mega tourist destination and a huge economic boom for Liberian and Black American investors as well.

The amazing thing about the Liberia coastline is that it literally has the culture and visible marks of Black Africans who created the first modern Black democracy in the world. How remarkable it would be for young Black children to visit places were their ancestors once stood and made their mark on history at a time when most of Europe did not know of or had not yet experienced democracy? Not making the social, economic, cultural, historical and educational connection between the descendants of Black Americans and their indigenous brothers and sisters in Liberia was a lost opportunity for the Doe administration. Sadly, the same mistake is still being made by other administrations that have come after Doe. His administration's bold plan was focused on erecting market buildings or centers. His desire to build market halls was influenced by the fact that his wife was a marketer before becoming the first lady of Liberia. Mrs. Nancy Doe had no formal education of any kind when her husband took over as head of state of Liberia. She was just an ordinary woman selling mostly farm crops and products in market centers to help support her family.

To Mrs. Doe's credit, just like her husband, she became an astute adult learner. As the years went by, she transformed herself from not knowing any English words, not even Librarian College English, to delivering polished speeches and hosting foreign dignitaries at events. She became a transformational face for all indigenous women and girls, not only in Liberia, but also for the marginalized indigenous populations around Africa.

Despite his own personal educational accomplishments and that of his wife, Samuel Doe had no interest in building or revamping the Liberian school system that would have met the literacy needs of the natives, who were mostly illiterate. Not only did he not have an interest in building or improving the educational system of the poor masses, his administration engaged in razor-sharp action to close schools and universities he accused of supporting dissident groups against his administration. This behavior on the part of Doe was criticized by many well-known educators as educational sabotage and mimicry of the native people, whose chances of education were being impeded by one of their own. For example, Doe waged war on schools like Tubman High, Dtweh and the University of Liberia.

In Doe's viewpoint, these schools were a breeding ground for political dissent against his administration's abuse of power. With no funding from his administration to pay teachers and support the Monrovia School System, teachers were forced to come up with unscrupulous behaviors such as selling the answers to test questions and the printing of pamphlets and forcing students to buy, or they were not allowed in class. Some of the teachers participated in the scammed to save their job and some were unscrupulous by nature. Some teachers would purposefully make the test difficult so that students would not find it easy to pass no matter how hard they studied. For those students who were very smart, they barely escaped the corrupt hands of those corrupt teachers. Meanwhile, many students who needed help had to depend on their pocketbooks to pass their tests. The Doe administration would often excuse oppositional leaders for inciting student riots; his administration would then use that as justification for the closure of leading public schools.

Unfortunately, for the indigenous people, this blatant attack on places of learning by one of their own was tantamount to suicide, because these schools mostly catered to the indigenous populations whose parents didn't have the money or resources to send them to private institutions. The president and his corrupt government officials, along with Liberian children from wealthy families attended private schools.

(The Brutal Death of Samuel K. Doe)

Meanwhile, by September 9th, 1990 Liberian were experiencing a full-scale war especially for those living in and around the capital Monrovia. As the warring factions slugged it out for territorial control of the nation's resources and strategic locations, Samuel Doe and the soldiers loyal to him began to quickly lose ground and important landmarks to a faction led by Prince Johnson, a former soldier of the Armed forces of Liberia and a comrade of the late Gen. Thomas Quwonpa. As the two forces battled for control of Monrovia, Johnson and his INPFL forces surrounded Samuel Doe inside the compound of the National Port Authority, where he was eventually captured and later decapitated by Johnson's fighters at his rebel base in Cardwell outside of Monrovia.

The events leading to Doe's invitation to the Freeport Authority of Monrovia is still unclear. However, after the capture of Samuel Doe, Johnson could be heard on his radio calling, "Tango-tango-tango, come in, over," leading many to believe that he was calling the American embassy to inform them that the mission was complete. After the capture and execution of Samuel Doe, the Liberian conflict went on to last for nearly 14 years, killing more than, 200,000 people and displacing nearly 500,000 people in refugee camps around the continent.

(The Master minder Charles G. Taylor)

Photo by: Alvin L. Sich

In the intervening period, the man who masterminded the Liberian civil wars is Charles G. Taylor, who is currently serving prison time in The Hague for related war crimes in neighboring Sierra Leone. Taylor, a corrupt former official of the Doe government, was charged with embezzling millions of dollars from the Liberian government. By the request of the Doe' administration, he was detained at a jail in Boston, Massachusetts awaiting a court hearing for his extradition to Liberia to face charges.

Unfortunately for the Doe administration, the United States never fulfilled its obligation to extradite Taylor to Liberia to face the Liberian people. Rather, the United States government informed the Liberian government that Mr. Taylor absconded from jail. America, with all its sophisticated monitoring systems, wanted Liberia and the world to believe that Charles Taylor, a half African Liberian man somehow managed to escape an American jail and jumped on a plane, subsequently ending up in Libya as a surrogate of Muammar Gaddafi. This remains a mystery to ordinary Liberians. The only conclusion that has settled in their minds regarding the Taylor saga is that the United States government or powerful individuals within it had a part to play in Charles Taylor's escape from jail.

Taylor, who was born to an Americo-Liberian father and a native Liberian mother, was not heard of after escaping jail in the U.S. until December 24,

1989. Taylor, along with other former officials from the Doe government turned rebel commandos along with a gang of exiled Nimbians from the Gio and Mano tribes, who surreptitiously made their way across the Liberian Ivorian borders, killing border guards and immigration security forces to launch a bloody incursion. Taylor's December 24, 1989, event introduced one of the bloodiest and most tragic periods in Liberia that would go on to have ripple effects on two of its neighboring countries, Sierra Leone and the Ivory Coast. The entry of Taylor and his rebel forces in Liberia brought about a tragic phase in the history of the African continent, particularly the West African sub-region. As Charles Taylor's rebel incursions spread in many parts of Liberia, other rebel groups began to form and enter senseless wars.

As countless rebel groups battled each other they left behind untold amounts of atrocities, such as the systematic raping of females, torture and summary executions of civilians, and anyone accused of supporting the opposition side. Unfortunately for the nation of Liberia, it lost many of its youth in the carnage, either through enslavement or forced entry into the military as child soldiers. Sometimes they were forced to take high-performance intoxicants and were made to killed. In the course of the nearly 14 senseless years of Liberian civil wars, its promising younger generation, some of whom were second graders, or still nurtured under their parents' watchful eyes, were made to dress up in filthy women's wigs and forced to carry AK-47s that were taller than their small underdeveloped frames. Many traveled for days and sometimes weeks or months, overly exhausted from the lack of proper nutrients and long hours walking in the tropical Liberian heat.

Liberia's future generation turned young killers were made to carry out atrocities against their own families and childhood friends in order to prove their quick and false acceleration into so-called manhood. Meanwhile, as these innocents were being turned into child killers, their so-called commanders and rebel leaders such as Taylor, Johnson, Kromah, and others feasted and drank wine in the comfort and safety of their air-conditioned homes, protected by groups of bodyguards. These so-called rebel commanders were soulless. They found no wrong in turning five- and 10-year-old children into killers. Sadly, for the youngsters recruited through raids or captured, some were made to eat the organs of their victims as part of a Black magic or voodoo ritual, believing that it would make them brave while putting their young undeveloped bodies in front of RPGs and machine gun rounds. Meanwhile, many of the so-called freedom fighters, high on drugs, burned down villages and towns in their paths as they made their way into the capital city of Monrovia. Illiterate, ignorant and physically underdeveloped, many of these young fighters were bamboozled into believing that they were fighting for a cause that would lift them up from the cruel hands of poverty, illiteracy and ignorance and deliver them into the wealth enjoyed by their so called rebel leaders.

Meanwhile, these mind manipulators of the indigenous youth had their own children and families living in safe capital cities around the world while they were engaged in siphoning proceeds from looted diamonds, gold, and timber, along other minerals into their foreign bank accounts abroad. As these heartless social hustlers were amassing their wealth overseas, the youth of Liberia were being prostituted, indoctrinated, heavily sedated with drugs and used as slave laborers in illegal diamond and gold mines they ran to enrich and fund their senseless wars. Given the history behind the establishment of the Liberian nation, tribal and ethnic conflicts were inevitable. The genesis of the Liberian conflicts had their roots buried deep in the creation of America and would later transfer to the small colonies that it helped to established for its freed Black slaves. The freed Black American settlers were unable to realized that no national minority group can systematically rule over the majority and expect no blowback, especially when the majority are being repressed and deprived of their basic rights.

The history of the world teaches us that over time the suppressed majority always fights back in the end to claim their rightful places. Despite the sequence of events in the history of Liberia, it delights me to say that all is not lost; the fight for the perfection of democracy is a long road that has many curves and bends along the way. The United States, which helped to establish Liberia, had its long narrow drive toward democracy and its share of ugly times. During the United States' journey toward the perfection of its democracy, many groups were left behind. Just until recently in the middle of the 19th century, women were not allowed to vote in America, and segregation was the law in many states in the Union. Things began to ameliorate not too long ago during the civil rights movement in the 1960s.

I hope that as we come to understand and appreciate our history and our connectivity, Americo- Liberians, Congolese Liberians and the indigenous African Liberian generation will galvanize their resources—both human, economic, technological, cultural and political—and start the work of building Liberia into the promised land that is supposed to be for the Black race, especially those descendants of Black American slaves.

We must understand that our forefathers dreamed of a Black-owned land that was established despite the underlying brutal conditions that were applied to them. Yes, they made a terrible mistake by excluding their indigenous African brothers and sisters from the affairs of the new nation Liberia, but it must be noted that this omission was not completely their fault. The prison of slavery had a lot to do with how they viewed themselves and how they viewed their African brothers. We, the descendants from both sides of the continent, can embrace their mistakes and learn from them and from there began to build, reminding ourselves that their work has not ended. I will also caution Americo-Liberians, Congolese Liberians and African (indigenous) Liberians that it was because of the love of liberty and the pursuit of happiness that drove our forebears to settle into this land now called Liberia, so let us work together and make them and our future generations proud.

CHAPTER 12

LIBERIA'S LONG JOURNEY TO DEMOCRACY

Photo by: Alvin L. Sieh

The arrival of the 21st century gave Liberians the feeling they had finally arrived at democracy. All too soon that feeling was replaced by obstacles from powerful and nefarious forces working among its citizens. Today, if you look at what is going on around the world, especially in Western capitals it is doubtful at the hope of democracy's promise to the world.

Countries that once seemed as promising democratic nations are slipping back surreptitiously toward dictatorships and authoritarianism. The hope and promise of democracy for the world once stood on the shoulders of those nations held down by communism and authoritarianism heading toward democracy and Human Right. As communism collapsed on itself from many corners of the globe, many celebrated the emergence of liberal democracy for the rest of the world. The 19th century witnessed a sea of nations paving the paths pointing toward freedom, liberty, and democratic principles. However, despite what might be called democracy in retrograde, it is worth mentioning that all is not yet lost for democracy that has long been hoped for. Today around the globe there are more democratic nations existing than at any time in the history of humanity, though it might not seem like it when you turn on the television or login to the internet for news.

According to Freedom House, a non-profit group engaged in tracking democracy around the world, there were 11 democratic nations in 1900, 20 in 1920, 32 in 1970, 77 in 2000 and 116 in 2018. As these statistics show, this represents strong progress toward the promise of democracy and should be welcomed with optimism and hopefulness. In a closely interconnected world, it is hard not to point to leaders who are giving in to domestic nationalist sentiment voicing their anger that democracy should be completely extinguished from the world. These voices are fueled by domestic economic, religious, ethnic and political upheaval in their respective countries.

Today in many parts of Africa the population is more interested in democracy than at any other time in the history of the continent. Africa's growing young population is more literate and rapidly interconnects with the rest of the world. These young people are more prosperous and politically savvy than the generation before them. With the internet, globalization, and the free flow of people across African borders, Africans are becoming much closer and better neighbors to each other. As a result of our nearness to one another, every citizen of the continent is directly or indirectly affected by the shockwave of events that occur at the borders of each other's countries due to the advancement of technology.

There are no denying that corrupt and distorted minds have wrongfully used the very technology that brings us closer to their advantage to bring discord and fracture our common space. These individuals are determined to prey on our diversity, connectedness and cooperative spirit, which is the life breath of democracy. Unfortunately for the supporters of democracy, these demagogues and propagandists of all kinds have effectively circulated across all borders at the speed of light, thereby endangering the orderly progress of democracy in the world. It hurts me to say that these dark-hearted manipulators have succeeded in swaying the weakest minds and the disconnected among us to believe in their discourse.

Meanwhile, it is worth noting that the inequality and some of the social ills that democracy creates has helped these demagogues to fuel the social problems that separate us. One does not need to look far to see how their actions have furthered social and political unrest in many parts of the globe. Today, Western capitals of the developed world that were once viewed by people in underdeveloped cities as bright shining symbols of thriving democracy are seen as being held hostage to hate and fearmongering against immigrants and those whose skin colors don't look like their own.

Sadly, for the growing fans and supporters of democracy, leading personalities with large microphones and strong social media platforms in majority Western capitals, are actively appearing on various platforms that promote their malignant views of democracy. Some of these fearmongering leaders can be seen in their various political capitals and social platforms, emitting hate and insults toward those who challenge their malignant viewpoints.

It is true that democracy has not always had an easy task in meeting the needs of the masses. I am certainly not interested in giving liberal democracy a smooth path. Democracy has generally come to light after the end of a difficult process, sometimes with immeasurable missteps and sometimes with measurable failures along the way. The architects and supporters of democracy must realize that it's always been easier to unseat dictatorships and tyrannical regimes than to construct a vibrant, functioning, and long-lasting democracy that promises social justice, equality and the protection of the rights of its citizens under the rule of laws. It is no time for those supporting democracy to fall asleep. Democracy often takes a long struggle to perfect. Some of the world's most ardent supporters of democracy went through long struggles to be where they are today. Those who are admirers of democracy have more work to do in perfecting their democratic vision.

Most fans and supporters of democratic systems see them as true symbols for the rest of the world to follow. However, American and European democracies did not come about by accident. It did not become a true symbol of liberal democracy until the second half of the 20th century. Most of America's southern states were under tyrannical regimes during the seventeen and eighteen hundred, and it would require a bloody civil war to demolish the tyrannical oligarchy which held that nation hostage for so long.

The rights of all Americans did not come about until another century passed before the federal government was capable of ensuring that all citizens in the union, including African Americans—who initially were held as slaves and had no rights to citizenship—could finally claim their rights as free people and exercise its freedoms. Despite the federal government's acknowledgment of citizens' rights for all Americans, there were segments of the population whose rights remain infringed upon by the very system that was supposed to ensure their protection. Unfortunately for many Americans, it would require more bloodshed and violent struggle for democracy to finally be guaranteed to all Americans.

Meanwhile, through the struggle for democracy, the American civil rights movement was born. The movement spearheaded the demand for racial qualities and guarantee of rights for all Americans regardless of race, gender, status, sexual orientation or religious preference. Some of these rights were achieved for most Americans less than a century ago, which is shameful for a country that prides itself on having one of the oldest human rights records in the world. However, despite American accomplishments in its struggle toward democracy, there remain deep political, geographical, economic, religious, tribal and social divides that continue to drive American social and political discussions with American citizens digging in their heels on both sides. To make matters worse for the fans of liberal democracy, the likes of Donald Trump, Marine LePen, Narendra Modi, Benjamin Netanyahu, Boris Johnson, and others of the world are seizing on the imperfections and failures of democracy and using our political and social debates to undermine the very democratic systems from which they received elevation to power and wealth.

When supporters of democracy look around them, there is no shortage of malignant political leaders who strive to propagate the demise of the very foundations of our democratic institutions. These corrupt-minded politicians play on the infraction of democracy to promote their own narrow nationalistic and malignant views of the world. Regrettably, for one of the world's oldest and most admired democracies, President Donald Trump is one of the leaders in this fight toward the demise of democratic principles. Because he is the president of the most admired democracy, whatever he says resonates around the world with leaders of the same inimical views of democracy.

President Trump, in one of his Trumpian statements, described African countries as "shitholes" and proclaimed he would prefer immigrants from western European countries to come to America than these "shithole African countries." What Donald J Trump is ignorant about is that he has no clue that there are about 5,000 Nigerian medical doctors today in the United States currently practicing, and that does not account for the second or third generation of Nigerians doctors in this arena. Today 29 percent of Nigerian- Americans over the age of 25 hold a graduate degree, compared to 11 percent of the overall U.S population according to the Migrations Policy Institute. In one of his racist remarked, Trump reportedly said in an Oval Office discussion that Nigerians would never go back to "their huts" once they saw America. Nigerian are emerging as one of the U.S most successful immigrant communities, with a median household income of $62,351, compared to $57,617 nationally as of 2016, according to the Migrations Policy Institute. As a gifted demagogue, Trump also referred to the hard-working people of Mexican heritage as "rapists and gang members." As for the desperate and displaced refugees of Syria, he compared them to "rabid dogs." As mentioned earlier, these are not just American or Trump originating problems. The spiteful dehumanization of a groups of people extends into some of the most respected capital cities in some of the world's leading democratic nations. This leads me to wonder whatever happened to the global excitement and optimism that elated and absorbed the world after the removal of the wall that separated East and West Germany in 1989. After the fall of this great wall, western democracy and its capitalist market system were excitedly embraced by supporters of democracy in every remote corner the world, as well as those whose hopes of democracy in parts of the world that was considered a dead dream.

As Western democracy and its capitalist market system gave hope to so many around the world, most of the world saw with excitement the unrestricted rise of so many out of poverty and political enslavement. Out of the blessings and openhandedness of western democracy and its capitalist market system came the birth of the global internet. The global internet brought the world closer at a speed unimaginable to many around the world, especially to those in remote places of the globe. This new technology created a new wave of global power, giving voices and power to people, helping to determine who and how they should be governed. The global net empowered ordinary people who usually did not have a voice in the affairs that governed them. With the blessing of this technology, the voices of ordinary people can no longer be ignored. Before the advent of this global connectedness, the global elites and political class systematically stepped away from the plights of the masses, especially the poor masses.

Because of this new western internet technology, rural farmers, social environmentalists and political activists from all parts of the world—some from places unheard of—are now coming together to effect change in all facets of global problems. Some have successfully removed undemocratic governments from power by uniting under one cause. Rather than championing the embrace of western democracy and its free-market system in places like Africa, India, Asia, the Middle East, and Eastern Europe, these demagogues are using their wealth and influence to endanger the orderly democratic process that helped make them wealthy. However, because of the stewardship and sturdiness of the democratic system, these demagogues and slanderers have successfully become millionaires and billionaires, and they continue to amass more wealth than 90% of the population. It is perplexing to see these benefactors of democracy living in the comfort and security provided to them by the very system they continue to malign. As a learned man, I am aware that most of these agitators are playing on the ignorance of the people on the lower end of the economic ladder.

Because these politically savvy individuals cannot deliver on the empty promises they make to their supporters, they cleverly divert our attention to things that divide us rather than to things that unite us as people of one human race. For example, if a pandemic or civil conflict erupt in any corner of our planet, it has a way of affecting the entire global market system in some fashion or form. Yes, we are all citizens of different countries, but as human beings, we are all citizens of the same planet; therefore, it is in the interest of everyone to work toward those causes that truly unite us.

For the very survival of global democratic systems, it is imperative that supporters and architects of the free market system begin examining with laser focus eyes on the capitalist market system that drives the world democratic system and the free market. We all need to question why is it that capitalism, has contributed to modern advancement and lifted so many out of poverty, yet the system has kept so many more in poverty and inequality, especially in some of the world's wealthiest nations. However, this may seem like a hard question to answer, because it will involve finger-pointing at the people who the major benefactors of the capitalist systems are mostly. On the other hand, those who advocate that since capitalism has failed on its promised to deliver the masses from poverty and inequality, it's now time for the world's economy to adopt a new market formula to replace the best-known system that humanity has currently tried and embraced. The reality is that while this proposal is gaining purpose among many, especially those who continue to face the daily ugliness and social inequality of capitalism, including the lack of healthcare, lower pay, ill- prepared educational system, inferior housing and employment opportunities. In the birth places of the free market system, there is still a great deal of despair and hopelessness among people of all races and social status about the current stage of western free market formula.

However, while some of the hopeless citizens and political agitators of the wealthiest nations blame the capitalist market formula for their current economic and social degradation, they are unsure of how to replace the current system, and with what substitute. In the interim, the world watches perplexed as countries that once championed democratic governments retreat into tribal corners and fudge new relationships with dictators and authoritarian regimes.

Fortunately, some remain hopeful for democracy in some of the unusual places in the world. Because of the advent of technology, many more citizens of the world are organizing and staging demonstrations to demand their rights, more so than in the past. Many more young people and even some of the elite ruling class and major benefactors of the capitalist systems are all marching the same avenues. They are demanding equality and fair democratic market systems that work for all people.

Fortunately, some upper-class elites understand that their existence and prosperity depend on the very survival and prosperity of their fellow citizens from poverty, social justice, and economic inequality. As a result, some of the rich elite classes are no longer bankrolling the political classes bent on destroying the democratic systems of their respective countries. Young men and women, along with some in the top upper class, are denouncing the nationalist voices that are making headlines in countries like Hungary, Brazil, France, London, Poland, Italy, the U.S., and other Latin American and Asian countries. In many parts of these countries, ordinary people are hungry for economic equality and social justice, and their sweat, tears, and blood are elevating them as they demand change, and they want it fast. This scenario is also playing out on the streets of many African countries. In Sudan, Algeria, Egypt and many other African capitals, the citizens who were oppressed are now demanding their economic freedoms from corrupt rulers.

The craving for a democratic system is on the rise in many African countries, as well as in Asia and Europe. For example, African countries, once noted for ushering into power the world's military strongmen, have been surprisingly active in electing democratic leaders in the past couple of decades. It is fair to question some of the democratic processes that brought some of these leaders into power. However, we can all agree that Africa, after centuries of colonial imperialist rule followed by years of military dictatorship regimes, is now on the precipice of working and perfecting democratic governance in many parts of the continent, partly because citizens are demanding it.

In the last few decades, West Africa has produced some of the best transfers of power from one democratically elected government to another in the whole history of the African continent. For example, Liberia, after facing devastating civil wars, peacefully elected its first female president and first female head of state on the African continent through a democratic process. Mrs. Sirleaf completed her two terms and peacefully transitioned her country from its dark war paths toward its current peaceful paths, she peacefully relinquished power to a new democratically elected successor. This marked the first recorded peaceful transition of power in the nation's history.

Additionally, Liberia's two next-door neighbors, who also suffered civil strife, have seen the successful transition of one democratically elected president to another without carnage or bloodshed. Unfortunately, the same cannot be said about the Middle East, Latin America and many other places that are considered developed or advanced developing nations of the world. Meanwhile, while there is no known alternative to the democratic and free-market system that we have come to adopt, we should not relent in continuing to examine the failure of our current system and fix the loopholes in our current economic model so that it can finally work for everyone. If we allow our current democratic and free-market system to work for all, we can undoubtedly drown out the voices of those demagogues and crusaders calling for the demise of democracy.

Photo by: Alvin L. Sieh

CHAPTER 13

THE TUMULTUOUS HISTORY OF WORLD DEMOCRACY

Photo by: Alvin L. Sieh

Liberia, like many other democracies around the world, has had a tumultuous transition period in the struggle toward perfecting its democracy. A brainchild of the United States, Liberia came to be when freed Black American slaves sailed to Africa in the pursuit of liberty and freedom. For over three hundred years they were held in bondage and denied the basic rights provided to man by his creator, including the rights to free speech, freedom to assemble, vote, pray to their creator and to be with those whom they love. All these rights are guaranteed by democracy. Ironically, while America was considered a democracy, it purposefully denied some of its citizens the basic rights that democracy provides and guarantees. It took American civil war and many other social events, including the civil rights movement, before democracy was fully possible and guaranteed to all citizens. The bitter fight for democracy is not only an American or Liberian experience. The United Kingdom, for example, which is often regarded as the birthplace of liberal democracy, had a turbulent struggle on the path to democracy.

To achieve democracy, the U.K. went through bloodshed and unrest leading up to the revolution of 1688. After that majestic revolution, it took centuries of hard work before the United Kingdom fully achieved true democracy during the early part of the 20th century. History also teaches us about some of the hard-fought struggles for democracy that started right in the heart of Europe.

In France, for example, the republic was declared in 1793, which was then considered the European continent's first modern democracy. The French achievement did not last long before crumbling into descent and terror. In the mix of French confusion and terror, a military coup was undertaken by General Napoleon Bonaparte. Under the military regime of Bonaparte, political and social instability engulfed France, which lasted all through the 19th century. It would cause France nearly five trials before finally being able to count itself a stable democracy in Europe, which came into being after World War II and after the French Algerian war of 1958.

Elsewhere in Europe, Italy, Spain, and Germany all struggled at ushering in democracy for its people. Meanwhile, as many European countries were struggling for stable democracy, Liberia was already enjoying democracy, which was imported from the United States. The democracy imported to Africa's oldest republic by freed Black Americans had its blemishes. It excluded the indigenous Africans from the democratic process. Just as it took the United States nearly a century-and-a-half after 1863 for it to recognize the rights of its Black citizens, it took Americo-Liberian nearly a century-and-a-half before recognizing the rights of the indigenous African Liberians they met in the settlements, which only came to fruition after a bloody coup that finally ended the Americo Liberians' dominant rules over the native majority.

Despite the demise of Black American dominance, Liberia was still not privileged or prepared to experience true, stable democracy until recently when its fourteen years of bloody civil war came to an end. In 2006 the Liberian people leaned on each other to try out democracy by voting in the first African female head of state and the nation's first woman commander in chief.
Mrs. Ellen Johnson Sirleaf took over the presidency after the nation emerged from divided and multi-ethnic tribal civil wars, which engulfed the Liberian nation in a reign of terror, senseless killing, and destruction. Before her

ascendancy, Mrs. Johnson Sirleaf had her own traumatic struggles with past administrations in her quest for the perfection of Liberia's shadow democracy.

She was once imprisoned in military prison among other male prisoners by the late president Samuel Doe. Sirleaf, unbroken by her past experiences, took over a country torn apart by nearly a decade-and-a-half of civil conflict that took the lives of nearly 300,000 of its people. She was taking over a nation in ruin from self-inflicted carnage. The nation's electricity, economic institutions, educational system, roads, bridges and other public sector infrastructures were burned down, or slowly decaying from years of neglect. Just as the first Black president in America was taking over a world economy that was in free fall, far away in Africa emerged the republic's first Black female president—Liberia's first woman president and Africa's first female head of state presided over a nation in total decay from the carnage of war.

For those critics who argue that Black people cannot handle a crisis, they need to reflect on the American experience under President Obama and the Liberian experience under Ellen Johnson Sirleaf. Mrs. Johnson Sirleaf took over Liberia's falling economy with an unemployment rate estimated at 70 to 75 percent according to UNICEF reports. After taking over as president, she reordered the nation's struggling national budgets from 84 million U.S. dollars to 300 million U.S. dollars a year in revenue increases. She used her superb international influence and credibility to renegotiate Liberia's nearly 4.8 billion dollars of debt that was run up by previous administrations.

The 14 years of civil war turned Liberia's once respected military and security forces into loyalists of various warlords. Liberia's military and security institutions became infected—a breeding ground for the corrupt tribal sentiment. In partnership with the United States, Ecowas and the UN, President Sirleaf was instrumental in the training and transformation of the military and security forces, returning them to their former respectable status. On the educational front, she was instrumental in the revamping of Liberia's three rural teacher training centers, which are currently in full operation.

With the help of the Chinese government, the University of Liberia moved into its new Fendall facilities outside of Monrovia. To make her government transparent, Sirleaf enhanced the role of the Auditing Commission and created the Liberian Anti-Corruption Commission (LACC), though her critics argued that the commission had not lived up to its task. In addition to her quest in improving the life of Liberia's degraded civil servants; she moved to increase their salaries as a means of discouraging public corruption. In further keeping the democratic process alive, the president, in partnership with UNIMIL, graduated nearly fourteen thousand men and women into the Liberian National Police force. One of President Sirleaf's greatest achievements, which most of her critics often forget, is her ability to promote and create safe corridors for free speech, freedom of the press and political dissent.

For the first time in Liberian history, critics of the president were able to broadcast over the airwaves to accuse and criticize the president, and yet go to bed safely, waking up alive without government security personnel knocking at their doors or the doors of their friends and family. Under Ellen Johnson Sirleaf's administration, Liberia witnessed the proliferation of dissenting voices against her foreign and domestic policies. Opposition parties and critics of the president could lament and assemble freely without fear of repercussions from the president or her security forces. Under President Sirleaf, the Liberian National Party for the first time operated in the heady atmosphere where they could challenge the president's policies without fearing that one of them would disappear or be imprisoned. Because she was able to keep Liberia's feeble democracy alive, it allowed aspiring political candidates to navigate freely about the country and present their cases to the Liberian people as to why they should be the one to replace her. As Liberian passion for democracy and the rules of law became inextinguishable, citizens became supercharged and turned out in waves to elect their next democratically elected president after President Johnson-Sirleaf's two terms ended successfully.

At a time when most of the world's leading or aspiring democracies were slipping back into political descent and authoritarian rule, Liberia once again made history by peacefully transitioning from one peaceful democratic administration to another. Under the stewardship of her Excellency, Mrs. Johnson Sirleaf peacefully handed over leadership from one political party leader to another, George M. Weah. To make the democratic process inclusive, she launched a massive voter education campaign targeting the interior and villages where most aspiring voters were uneducated about participating in democracy. It's noteworthy to mention that while many developed democracies were impeding the participation of their marginalized citizens in the democratic process, the Liberian government through its National Election Committee made a concerted effort to provide voter education and access to equal participation to all marginalized groups, including many who were voting for the first time in their lives.

Despite the enormous structural and logistical challenges, the commission maintained a commitment of training, mobilizing, informing, and sharing geared to empower marginalized groups who made up most of the nation's indigenous population. Under her astute political leadership and commitment to a peaceful transfer of power to her successor, Mrs. Johnson-Sirleaf turned over affairs of state to her successor, president-elect George Manneh Weah.

CHAPTER 14

THE GIFT OR THE MESSIAH?

Photo by: Alvin L. Sieh

After the proverbial iron lady of Liberia, Mrs. Ellen Johnson Sirleaf, dominated the leadership of the Liberian political front ending with 12 years of her two-term presidency, she resurrected Liberia's feeble democracy from its deathbed. By popular vote and demand from the Liberian voters, she peacefully handed the prescription for keeping the nation's young, fragile democracy alive to the new president-elect, George M. Weah. The fragile democracy needed the president's full and undivided attention, as well as the efforts of every well-meaning Liberian citizen, both at home and abroad, doing whatever it took to boost the health of the nation's democracy to keep it thriving.

The Liberian people needed full and unrestricted participation in the country's affairs, especially the indigenous groups that had long been barred from many of the nation's wealth and educational opportunities. The voices of both supporters and dissenters had to be heard to keep democracy alive and working for all citizens of the beautiful land of liberty.

As I hesitate to call the new president "Messiah," as many of his supporters did, there is full recognition that he is a gift to the Liberian indigenous people who, for a long time had no real voice in the affairs of the government. For the second time, Liberians had the opportunity to elect an indigenous president. The first time was in 1985, but the process was overshadowed by accusations of corruption, voter fraud, and abuse, which eventually led to carnage and terror, ushering in 14 years of bloody civil conflict. This time, things are different.

Undeniably, there has not been a better time than now to be a citizen of Liberia, and there has not been a better time than now to be president or head of state of any African nation. For nearly 400 years, Africa suffered a corrosive effect from the loss of its human capital, when over 20 million of its young and vibrant people were held in bondage and sold as slaves to western nations and elsewhere in the world. The African continent was left weak and diminished to defend itself against Western colonizers who later came back to exploit most its natural resources.

The returning Westerners used force and malignant methods ravage the continent's natural resources. As a result of this deep exploitation, these Western nations were able to lift themselves from poverty and backwardness into the age of enlightenment. For centuries, these colonizers used a distorted, corrupt system of government that benefited them and their puppet leaders, some of whom unfortunately came from among the very afflicted people that they were supposed to help.

There is no denying that because of the exploitation of Africa by all of the so-called former colonial countries as precipitated many young Africa trying to escape carnage, poverty, and disease by risking their lives on makeshift inflated rafts, only to end up in self-imposed slavery in Western countries where they are largely despised. Some citizens and leaders in these Western countries are proud to paint a jarring picture of these refugees as chaotic, violent people who should not be welcome on their shores. Some go so far as demonstrating in their pristine capitals to show their pathological hatred of foreigners, particularly African immigrants.

News flash for demagogues and hatemongers: the world is witnessing a sea change on the African continent. After losing most of its human population to slavery, disease and war, Africans are once again on the path to becoming the most populated continent in the world. As an African, I am delighted to see that Africa is back on the path to the regrowth of its rich human resource.

Africa is growing at the speed of light, outpacing every other developing continent in the world. While many European and Asian nations are substantially decreasing in population growth, African countries are substantially increasing in population growth. According to a recent UN forecast, in 1950 sub-Saharan Africa had just 180 million people. By 2050 it will have 2.2. Billion people—three times as many people as Europe. If the current UN forecast is correct, sub-Saharan Africa will have 4 billion people by 2100. In addition, Africa is expected to have the youngest population in the world. It is forecast that most of Africa's population will be younger than 20 years old. This massive population growth comes with both opportunities and challenges. The challenge to African leaders, including newly elected president George Weah of Liberia, is that they need to make sound policy proposals and decisions to turn the growing youth population into an asset to the continent and the world.

This assessment should draw the attention of African leaders and policymakers and spur them to start asking themselves crucial questions to hopefully come up with tangible solutions to address the issues of Africa's massive population growth. This population growth is not just a challenge for Africa alone. Developed nations can either sit back or continue to support outdated policies that have done nothing, or they can vigorously engage with progressive new leaders who are embracing economic, political and social enlightenment for their respective nations. In an interconnected world, unrest in the streets of Monrovia, Nairobi, Freetown, Mogadishu, Lagos and elsewhere in Africa has the potential to create unrest in the streets of Washington D.C, London, Paris, Rome, and elsewhere in world capitals.

Currently, the proliferation of migrants and refugees arriving on the shores of Europe and America is a prime example of failing to improve social, political and economic progress in nations with the fastest-growing populations, which can bring about political and social instability to developed nations separated by thousands of miles apart. If the world's so-called superpowers and African leaders think that they can place a bandage on the problem and hope it will solve itself, they would be ushering in what I believe would be the next global migration of desperate and afflicted people chasing hopeless dreams in western capitals around the world.

What Africa and its growing young populations need is not the infusion of more donations or foreign aid into the pockets of corrupt African leaders and corporate executives overseeing outdated organizations that are amassing balance sheets for their board members. We have tried these old and outdated methods in the past to address Africa's problems and it has never worked for the betterment of the masses. Donors and foreign aid breeds more ravenous corrupt plutocrats at the expense of the poor ignorant masses. It is my conviction that prosperity and growth for Africa will not be achieved from an unending flux of foreign aid and donor support. Rather, Africa's prosperity and growth will come through investing in innovations that create new market opportunities, unrestricted entrepreneurial ideas and the can-do, outside the box mindset.

With technological connectivity, it is now doable for a young entrepreneur in Monrovia to sell his products to potential customers in Ghana or Lagos via online marketplaces. It is now even possible for an unknown farmer to sell his product to a customer in New York or London. Today it is also achievable for a young activist to galvanize forces in all the formerly unreachable places on the continent in order to draw attention to important causes without the need to gather in a single location or group.

A good example is a young man in Nairobi who saw the proliferation of used plastic waste floating in Nairobi waterways polluting that country's ecosystem. Of his own volition, he decided to act via social media to capture the attention of his fellow countrymen. Through his undaunted effort and passion for a tangible solution, he caught the attention of the environmental ministry, which eventually led to the passing of legislation banning the use of plastic bag waste in Kenya. As you can see, technology and innovation precipitated this young Kenyan's outreach effort. Despite the lack of effort from most African leaders, advancement in technology and innovation has mitigated needless infrastructure development. For example, because of the development of cell phones and social media, most of Africa has been able to escape landline phone infrastructure in every corner, town, and village. This is something that if left with African governments, may not have happened for generations.

Another advancement in technology has made it possible to bring electricity to towns and remote villages using wind turbines. Solar energy, along with other new sources of electricity generates enough electricity for Africa to shine around the clock. Furthermore, with unimpeded use of the internet, Africans are now able to learn true facts about their part of the world. They have gained knowledge about their governments, character, and behaviors of the people who are representing them. The 21st century has brought so much potential for the African continent. This was published in a recent report and analysis from *The Economist* titled, "The New Scramble for Africa." *The Economist* reported that, "The first great surge of foreign interest in Africa, dubbed the first 'scramble' for Africa was in the early 19th century when European colonial powers carved up the continent and seized African land to divide it among themselves.

The second "scramble" for Africa was during the Cold War when East and West vied for the allegiance of newly independent African states. The Soviet Union was on one side, backing Marxist tyrants while America and its Europeans partners were propping up despots who claimed to believe in capitalism as a system of progress.

And finally, the third "scramble" for Africa, which is now underway, is more benign. Outsiders have noticed that the continent is important and becoming more so because of its growing population. By 2025, the UN predicts that there will be more Africans than Chinese people. Governments and businesses from around the world are rushing to strengthen diplomatic, strategic and commercial ties with African governments. These have the potential to create vast opportunities for the continent growing population. Today Africa recorded some of the fastest growing economic in the world and is set to have some of the largest cities in the world in a very few years. Today Africa is the largest user of mobile payment system in the world and growing. It has over 400 million more mobile phone user.

If African leaders handle these new "scrambles" wisely, the main winners will be African themselves. According to *The Economist,* there is a huge spark in foreign engagement and diplomacy in various African countries by big world powers and emerging economies. According to a UN briefing, from 2010 to 2016, more than 320 embassies were opened on the African continent, making it the largest foreign embassy building boom on any continent. China is currently the largest seller of military equipment and technologies to approximately 45 African countries. On the other hand, Russia has also planted itself on the continent by entering into military agreements with 19 African nations.

In pursuit of African glory, rich Arab nations are building bases on the

Horn of Africa and employing African mercenaries to deal with their extremist issues and the growing network of proxy wars. Elsewhere in Africa, Turkey has opened 26 embassies, while India is in the process of opening nearly 18 embassies in Africa. America, France, and Great Britain are expanding their reach because of competition from new players. Newly emerging economies such as Singapore and Indonesia are all rushing for a piece of the African pie.

If only smart African leaders and policymakers can visualize the potential of Africa's growth and size. Africa is well on its way to becoming a global marketplace, not only for itself, but also for the rest of the world. If we can avoid foreign exploitation from bribes that influence corrupt officials into signing shady deals that benefit not the masses but foreign investors and their corrupt leaders, we will be on our way to addressing the needs of our growing population. Unfortunately for the rest of Africa, there remains an abundance of corrupt African leaders and officials with foreign handlers waiting in the wings to launder money into European bank accounts. However, despite all these challenges, there is no better time than now to be a citizen of an African nation. It is equally true that there has never been a better time than now to be a head of state of any African nation.

Let us not be negligent in acknowledging that there are still enormous challenges ahead of us to be collectively overcome in order to reap the benefits of our new economic opportunities. All over the African continent there lie many self-imposed obstacles that have been created by past poorly educated, ignorant leaders who are impeding growth and development. Additionally, some of Africa's obstacles to growth and development were imposed by former African colonial power exploiters for their own benefit. Unfortunately for Africa, we still have flamboyant and bombastic social hustlers in our governmental corridors that are controlling important policy decisions and benefiting significantly from these failed policies, so they have no incentive to affect any positive and progressive changes that would advance the masses. However, despite the ill will of these corrupt leaders, I am optimistic and confident that as more young and old people demand change from the old, failed policies of the past, these corrupt leaders who indulged in elaborate lifestyles at the expense of the poor masses, may realize their days are numbering toward the end.

No longer can they hide the truth from the people, no longer they can break the will of the determining population yearning for change. The world has become a global mirror for all to view their own images, as well as the images of others. We can now see what is happening in each other's governmental cycles from a distance, and quickly draw attention to them just by the click of a button. An injustice from any corner of the globe can easily be seen by all, sometimes instantly through the capable laser focus of social media or the internet by the simple efforts of ordinary people around the world. It is also worth mentioning that while it's true that the internet and other forms of technological innovation have made it easier for us to move our world forward, it has also made it permissible for the ill-intentioned among us to easily split our world apart, create trouble and reshape the global order of things. There are no shortages of these people to be found, whether in some of the most powerful democratic places in the world, or in corrupt and repressive regimes.

Many of these bad actors are working hard to create discord using the very instruments that we cherish for bringing us together. Let us hope that the defenders and supporters of world peace, as well as globalists, never get overly sentimental by mundane achievements and fall asleep. As Africa braces itself for the third wave of its economic "scrambling" and its growing youthful population, Africans have to dig deeper to figure out how to ultimately usher out the old power and backward ideas while at the same time ushering in a new power that is open and transparent. This must be citizen involved, peer-to-peer driven and technically innovative without falling behind the curve. As Africa's young and energetic youth navigate in a hyper-connected world, they are going to need leaders who are pragmatic, transparent, straightforward and entrepreneurially/technologically driven. Those African leaders who are capable of pioneering people toward these ideas will no doubt be the leaders that history will remember and reward for spearheading the transformation of a new and youthful generation of African leaders.

Meanwhile, if Africa's new hyper generational innovators, entrepreneurs, and leaders are to reach their full potential, Africa must begin by eradicating the repressive structures left by its formal imperialist and colonial rules that are still in place in many African countries. It is a complete derangement to see that in the 21st century Africa, with all its educated people, has not been able to extricate itself from the grips of failed imperialist systems that has kept the continent backward for centuries. Most of Africa has been mentally buried and intoxicated by these rejected western systems that they inherited centuries ago and cannot let go of, simply because the systems benefit the powerful few holding onto power. It is now proven that incredibly old, failed western systems that we continue to hold are clearly not serving anyone well anymore. For example, the very economic systems that were uploaded from western institutions and adopted in Africa are currently failing their own citizens and sinking most western nations in piles of debt, economic and educational inequality, racial violence, marginalization of minority groups, homelessness, drug addiction, hate-mongering and racism. These are all parts of the social decay brought about by the failed systems that many African nations are tenaciously clinging to in order to address the problems of the 21st century on the continent.

In my birth country of Liberia, we are still holding onto old imperialist rules that were imported by the free Black Americans who founded the country. One example is the restriction of land ownership only to those with Liberian citizenship. With this backward policy, no foreign investors will be willing to make important, meaningful investments in Liberia if they are unable to own the land that they are operating on, except when they know that they are secretly benefiting more than expected. Another failed policy adopted from the westernized Black American founders is the restriction placed on the people to elect their county head or superintendent, which in America is like electing a governor. Under the current Liberian policy, the executive or president is the only person with the authority to appoint a superintendent. As such, the superintendent is answerable only to the president and serves at his pleasure, not at the pleasure of the people he oversees. Since Liberian superintendents are not elected by the people or voters, their main concern is to promote the president or his political party agenda, not the people.

Furthermore, the restriction of Liberian citizenship only to people of the Black race is another impediment holding back development, innovation, and growth. However, one can certainly understand the ideas that generated such a mindset in the first place. After the slaves were free to voyage to their ancestral land, they wanted to make sure that their former slave masters did not come after them and re-enslave them in their own colony. Therefore, they made laws that excluded anyone who was not Black from becoming citizens and owning land. These were the same restriction placed on them while they were in America both as slaves and as freemen and women. Meanwhile, at the time it must have been prudent for such restrictions to be imposed. However, holding onto such restrictions in the 21st century is not only unwise, but a bludgeoning tool forcing stagnation in both growth and economy. In a globally connected world, these ideas are no longer workable. Liberians have almost no restrictions in many parts of the world from owning land to becoming citizens.

So, the real question to be asked is why Liberian lawmakers are still holding onto outdated colonial restrictions of growth and development that are embedded in its constitution. It is time to ameliorate those racially divided policies that benefit only the few poorly educated lawmakers who protest their abolishment. In order to avoid another loss of centuries of human capital, current leadership in Liberia must begin by vigorously addressing and permanently eradicating the culture of laziness, begging, corruption, illiteracy, lawlessness and an "it's who you know" mentality.

Rather than hiring people in a position of trust based solely on who you know, our current leaders must begin to adopt a system of hiring people solely based on the individual's qualifications, experience, and character. We also must not place people in a position of trust if they are believed to have questionable character regardless of their accumulated degrees and certifications. If we are to maintain our striving democracy and prosperity, the next decade must focus strongly on hard work, honesty, and optimism rather than pessimism, and pro-growth, rather than pro-poverty. Decentralization of our government over a corrupt centralized system where the leaders are handpicked by a centralized bureaucracy instead of local people, this would be a major step in the right direction. In the next decade, our leaders should encourage a democratic market system over a single monopolized system where one individual is allowed to import and export major commodities of the nation just because he or she is sleeping comfortably in the pockets of corrupt officials in government. What such a single monopolized market system does to a thriving economy is to starve growth, innovation and competitiveness.

A single monopolized economic system allows handpicked businessmen and women to control scarcity and pricing at will, without any interference from those whose pockets and bank accounts are being uploaded. The next decade should be laser focused on developing new entrepreneurial attitudes, consumers of locally manufactured goods and products. Liberians should become innovators of ideas rather than observers of other people's innovations and productivity. The next decade should bring us to a place where the laws in our constitution and the judicial system really matter and are applied to all without prejudice, political status, and the influence of wealth. Laws should have the same meaning for Weah, Johnson, Kamara and the sons and daughters of Blamo, Mondaygar, and Flomo.

(Message to George Weah)

Mr. President, rather than ignoring our diaspora we should incentivize and encourage young people to resettle back home so that they can contribute their vast reservoir of talent to the rebuilding of our critical infrastructures in Liberia. We are extremely fortunate that our young people were educated in the various nations of the world in which they reside and are currently contributing to the development of their adopted countries. Liberia needs their experience to jump-start us in meeting the challenges of the 2035-2050 economic wheels that are set to roll into Africa.

One of the most important legacies of the tragic Liberian civil wars have been the creation of the modern Liberian diaspora that spread all over the world, especially in the United States, Canada, Europe, Asia, the Middle East and elsewhere. These vibrant Liberians of various ethnic backgrounds have had a considerable impact on the cultures of their various adopted nations, especially during the 20th century. They specialize in myriad fields—medicine, science and technology, economy, entrepreneurism, music, fashion, food and culinary arts, the arts, education, government services, the military, and law enforcement.

Liberia and other African countries are currently sitting on a gold mind of human capital that is not being utilized and welcomed. For example, there are those in Liberia who criticize the reintegration and expertise of the Liberian diaspora in the country's current recovery toward good leadership and economic advancement, often accusing them of leaving the country when it needed them the most. However, it is overly simplistic to suggest that the Liberian diaspora consists simply of a group of unpatriotic people who fled Liberia when it was most in need of them (including me) and returned when we are least needed. The truth is that Liberian diaspora are more needed now than any other time in history. We are a diverse, multifaceted and multigenerational demographic spanning every socioeconomic background. Many Liberians left the country or were raised abroad for a variety of reasons, including civil wars, ethnic conflict, insecurity or simply the lack of educational and economic opportunities.

Yet despite the distance created through no fault of their making, many hold close and personal relationships with their beloved country and their family, either through regular visits, establishing transnational business ties and remittances of money amounting to millions of dollars. In fact, some estimate the amount to be in the billions of dollars and most of those remittances have been uploaded into the Liberian economy at a time when the international community had stopped putting money into the government of Liberia. These remittances helped to support livelihoods and economic development, but they were not the only contribution coming from the Liberian diaspora.

Today in Liberia many small businesses came into existence because of the contributions of the Liberian diaspora and many of these businesses are operated by family members living at home, creating employment and helping to reduce Liberia's alarming unemployment rate. Additionally, when the Ebola disaster struck the homeland, many of these diaspora became crucial lifelines to those Liberians affected by the Ebola virus, by sending money, medications, messages and instructions on preventive steps to stop the spread of the virus to family members and friends helping to put a stop to it.

Through outreach efforts in the United States and around the world, Liberian diaspora were able to raise awareness among ordinary citizens of their respective countries and galvanized resources from those citizens to send in volunteers, along with materials and financial support to the desperate people of Liberia. In testament to their love for their homeland, many diasporas in the medical and emergency management fields risked their lives for their fellow citizens by abandoning their comfortable lifestyles to race to the middle of the pandemics to help their brothers and sisters in Liberia.

Liberian diasporas are helping shape Western policy agendas and offer a better model of foreign and regional financial and technological support to the homeland. It is now urgent and necessary for today's Liberian government under George Weah to engage with the diasporas by realizing that their power and influence is critically needed for the betterment of Liberia and its current government. In many other African countries and emerging countries, the potential of their diaspora is recognized and prioritized as legitimate stakeholders in the future development of their respective nations. It is now time for Liberia to recognize the talent and potential of its diaspora. Liberia has potential to be the next big place where innovation, creativity and entrepreneurship spring forth. However, we cannot achieve any of that if we do not collectively confront the evil, dark hands of corruption head-on. In our nation's history corruption has become a national spectator sport for which players are rewarded with more government jobs and contracts.

The summary failure of laws and a functioning judiciary system is the fuel that gives birth to corruption in any society. Corruption is a serious threat to democracy and human decency. It has robbed the people of Liberia and most of Africa of their dignity and opportunity for a better life in a dignified world. Fighting corruption has afforded the people of Liberia and other African nations the chance for better schools, hospitals, healthcare, food, security, and better infrastructure.

Look around you and watch world news reports—corruption has enabled desperate Africans to make dangerous journeys over the high seas to seek a better life in places they are not wanted. For unknown reasons corrupt leaders and their nefarious supporters are too blind to the plight of their fellow citizens to change the corrupt system they preserve.

Mr. George Weah based on the timing of your election, I am of the undaunted hope that you are the right man for the job of president of the republic of Liberia. You are a crossover between the millennial generation and the old school generation of Liberians. The millennial views you as one of them, despite the age gap. Nearly every 18-year-old and under-30 adult voted for you overwhelmingly in your incredible election. Their overwhelming support and admiration for you is triggered by their love for the game of soccer, a game that you perfected during your time on the world stage.

Soccer is the only game in town and a golden ticket out of the slums for most poverty-stricken Africans youth. They admire the man who is the embodiment of success through the game that most under-privileged kids dreamed about around the world. Mr. Weah, you are a true example of a man whose success in life came from playing soccer, one of the most popular sports known to most on the African continent. No other African soccer players had the remarkable achievement and records in the game as you did. George Weah is undoubtedly a lightning rod for Liberian youth, and a proud symbol of Africa. Additionally, Weah is also an embodiment of what hard work dedication, and perseverance can achieve.

For some he is the perfect role model of a focused and determined man, whose journey to the top of the world soccer map, along with other personal and professional accomplishments, came with hard work and dedication to his country.

Born George Manneh Weah on October 6, 1966 in Monrovia, Liberia, Weah's early life was marked by hardship while growing up in Clara Town, a poor slum suburb of Monrovia, with his late maternal grandmother, whom he loves dearly and often parades on the world stage for all to see after making his name and fortune. Under his grandmother's loving guidance, young George lived a normal and happy life, always respectful of others and cheerful despite the challenges that life threw at him and his family. According to close friends of the Weah family, young George, or Manneh a name his late grandmother preferred to call him, would often time go to bed with just one meal in his belly. Manneh (or Oppong, as he was famously called), had a unique talent that was hidden in his feet, which the whole country and the world would come to discover, that would pilot him to the higher echelons of the world soccer stage.

George Weah's soccer talent was discovered when he began playing barefoot on uneven, grassless fields in the slum of Clara Town in Monrovia. He would later move on to play the game he dearly loved in high school and on community fields around Monrovia, where his path to stardom began to take shape. As George began to play around Monrovia's grassless fields, everyone wanted to have him on their teams, especially when it was discovered that he had a unique way of possessing the ball between his legs and double dribbling his opponents, leaving them behind him in the dust.

Defenders and goalkeepers where terrified by his athletic ability and speed. Manneh was always on the winning side with his unique ability to score goals from nearly any position on the soccer's field. Soon word of Weah's talent began to spread like wildfire, and news of his talent was spread throughout the streets and slums of Monrovia and its surrounding area. It did not take too long for prominent soccer teams to start auditioning him for his talent.

Key among the teams competing for George Weah's talent were the Mighty Barrolle Football Club, a first division team in Monrovia. In his first year with the team in 1985, he made sure that his talent and soccer skills were an asset to the Mighty Barrolle Football team by scoring much needed and decisive goals. Unfortunately, for the Barrolle Football Club, Weah's stay with the team was brief before the team's rival, the Invisible Eleven "IE" Football Club lured him with gifts and others pursued him to join their teams, leaving intense dislike between him and officials, along with fans of his former team for decades.

While playing for the Invisible Eleven "IE" team his athletic prowess was again on display for the nation to see, as he scored critical goals and made important plays for his teammates. By the end of the soccer season, Manneh Oppong Weah was, the highest goal scorer on the team, propelling team "IE" to clinch the national league title. As a result of his high performance and display of natural talent on the field, coaches on the Liberian National team Lone Star came knocking, urging him to play on the national team. For Weah, this was a high honor that not many players received.

Without hesitation, Weah answered the call to duty and joined the Liberian

Lone Star team. With George Weah on the Liberian national squad the Lone Stars, along with other talent like James Debbah, Joe Nagbah and others, the Lone Stars of Liberia became a serious contending force in African soccer arenas. Weah's first international goal came against the fearsome Green Eagles of Nigeria, which was a big affair at the time.

Weah's show of talent and hard work on the soccer fields soon caused him to be noticed by professional coaches from Tonnerre of Yaoundé during an international African club game in Monrovia against his club. Soon after that match, George Weah signed his first international professional soccer contract with Tonnerre in 1987. Blessed with a natural talent, Weah had a short stay in Cameroon with Tonnerre, and landed the club and the Cameroonian National Club league title. The fans of Tonnerre of Yaoundé wanted more of the amazing and undisputable soccer talent of Weah for their next season.

The Cameroonian coach Claude Leroy quickly recognized the unique, impressive talent in Weah and was convinced that Cameroon was not the place to absorb the unquestionable soccer skills of this son of Liberia. Coach Claude concluded that Weah needed a much bigger stage to display the natural dribbling and shooting skills he possessed. That same year after the end of the season in Cameroon, coach Leroy persuaded Weah to advance and take his soccer talent on the French stage. With his determination and humbleness, Weah took the advice of his coach and moved to France in 1987. While in France, Weah signed a lucrative contract with the A.S. Monaco Football Club.

Weah, a young boy who grew up in a poor Liberia slum, who learned to play the game of soccer without the input of any soccer trainer or coach, soon found himself playing the game he loved in one of the world's most prestigious soccer league, the European Soccer League. However, while in France playing for A.S Monaco, Weah scored 57 goals, helping his team to clench the French league championship in 1991. Weah spent five years with A.S. Monaco before moving on to play for another French soccer giant, Paris Saint Germain.

George Weah was now living in Paris, the French capital, as the result of his talent. Back in Liberia, no one in their right mind would have thought that a poor young Liberian boy raised in the slums playing soccer barefoot on dusty, uneven fields around Monrovia would end up having an illustrious soccer career that would land him on one of the world's most beautiful cities on earth. I urge you to please think about this before you read about his other fine accomplishments.

While playing for Paris St Germain, he led his club to the French league championship and to the semifinal of the 1995 European Championship League. However, after nearly three seasons with PSG another heavyweight European team came in search of his incredible talent, which give him dominance over defenders and goalkeepers of opposing teams.

By 1995, the Italian soccer giant, A.C. Millan, signed George Weah to another lucrative soccer contract. Weah again moved to another beautiful European city and surrounded by wealth, something he did not know existed while growing up dirt poor in the slum of Clara Town. With his new team, Weah once again showcased his incredible talent to Italian soccer fans and showed what he was made of. While playing for A.C. Millan, Weah proved once again his masterly skill on the Italian soccer stage by leading his club to two championships titles in 1996 and again in 1999.

One would be wrong to think that after all these impressive accomplishments, Weah's success story was at an end. In fact, it was the opposite; his greatest accomplishments still lay ahead of him. The fact that Weah is not famously talked about and lionized in the soccer world as one of the best that ever played the game is startling, but that doesn't surprise me as an African or a Black man living in the west.

Through my search for knowledge I have come to realize that usually Black Africans are talked about less frequently in the world press; their achievements are often buried under the table in the world's press rooms. It is sad to say, but we African do not do enough to tell our own stories to the world. We Africans are fond of retelling the stories of the white man or other races more vigorously than telling our own stories of accomplishment to the rest of the world with pride. Until we can begin to tell our own stories of accomplishment and lionize our own heroes, the rest of the world will continue to portray us as a people who have not contributed enough toward the advancement of humanity.

In 1995 while playing for the Italian club, George Weah grabbed the soccer world's attention. Because of his unparalleled and incredible, humble talent, he was named the world's best soccer player. In addition, he was also named Europe's best player and Africa's best football player, all in the same year. George Weah is the first and subsequently remains the only African soccer player to have achieved such a prestigious accomplishment. What made George Weah's story unique and incomparable to any other athlete is that he achieved all these milestones while having to deal with brutal, ethnic civil wars in his homeland, Liberia. Like many Liberians, Weah lost many loved ones, families and friends to the Liberian carnage.

During the height of the civil war conflict the Liberian national team, Lone Star, had its commitments to play in both the African and World's cup qualification rounds. With the various warring factions duking it out, no safe places remained for the Lone Star team to conduct it practices. Weah, being the charitable man that he is, he paid for all the home base players, coaches and officials of the Liberian Federation Association to go to Accra Ghana, where the team stayed to practice for all its international obligations. Weah also helped facilitate the travel expenses of other professional and semi-professional players who were on the national team squads. Each time Weah traveled to the national team engagements, he would bring along team uniforms and equipment from sponsors in Europe for the Liberian national team to wear during matches.

George also frequented refugee camps in Ghana and the Ivory Coast, where nearly half a million Liberians escaping from the war at home were taking refuge. During some of the Liberian games or matches in the Ivory Coast or Ghana, he purchased tickets for hundreds of Liberian refugees to attend games to watch and cheer their Lone Star team. Weah knew that the games of sport were the instrument that brought Liberians together during the country's divided ethnic civil wars. Watching those games allowed Liberians escape the strife happening around them and to remember the good old days when they used to come out in unison to cheer their national team. They were proud watching their European and African based professional players who represented Liberia's good image abroad, which took their minds off its image as a war-torn nation.

While everything coming out of Liberia had been negative and depressing at the time, George Weah and his fellow professional soccer stars playing overseas were the only proud accomplishment that Liberians could point to. I remember walking into a takeout food place in Trenton, NJ, and when the owner heard my accent, he proceeded to ask me where I was from. Once he heard Liberia, his face lit up and his eyes opened wide, exposing their beautiful brown color. "George Weah is the best!! PSG all the way," the man gushed in his heavily deep Arab voice. It turned out that he was from Egypt and a die-hard supporter of PSG. As I was about to pay for my chicken wings, he smiled and gestured to the cashier, who turned to me and said, "Keep your money, eat free!"

Because of George Weah's generosity and his ability to unite all segments of Liberian society through his gifts and talent, the United Nations picked him as a Goodwill Ambassador to help lead Liberia's fragile peace process and reconciliation efforts. However, as Liberia's warring factions were still armed and blood thirsty, Weah risked his life as the goodwill ambassador, travelling to Liberia on several occasions. Weah allied with the UN and Ecowas peace monitors to rally Liberian warring factions toward disarmament, peace and reconciliation. Many young rebel fighters yielded to his call, which helped lead the way toward disarmament and peace in Liberia. As George Weah, became visible and passionately supporter of peace in Liberia, many admirers of his work encouraged him to take a deep look at running for the presidency. Because he was the most popular and well-known Liberian without blemish against his character and untainted by any events associated with the war, many supporters, fans, politicians and donors, along with an overwhelming segment of Liberian society saw him as the best person to lead Liberia out of its dark and bloody past. By then, George Weah was retired and living in the United States with his wife and children.

Countless people began to encourage him to step into politics. Weah was aware of his popularity with the indigenous majority, particularly the youth who outnumbered the adult population in Liberia, and soon enough his level of education and understanding of geopolitics came to the fore. These questions came from his critics, most of whom saw his popularity with youth as a major benefit for him and a major obstacle for them if he were to run. With his unyielding determination to overcome obstacles and achieve major milestones, Weah took a big jump into his future career, which set the stage for what came next in his remarkable career. As a father, husband and champion for the underclass, Weah was not hindered by those responsibilities when he enrolled in a four-year online college in the USA.

After four years of rigorous academic study, he graduated with a bachelor's degree in public administration, thereby addressing one of the flaws his critics were quick to use against him. On the other hand, no one could question his patriotism, his wealth, his ability to mobilize the Liberian people, or his generosity to his fellow citizens. As much as his critics liked to point to his lack of higher education as a weakness or his ability to run a country, his supporters were quick to point back to his critics, reminding them that George Weah was the only Liberian who was a legitimate millionaire, not earning his wealth through corruption or stealing from the poor, as many running against him had done.

After obtaining his degree in 2005, Weah decided to test the Liberian political landscape by declaring his intention to run for president of Liberia. George Weah was bringing with him something that most of the politicians running against him did not have, which was his name. The name George Oppong Manneh Weah was a household name, not only in Liberia, but all over the African continent. He also brought character credibility that most of those running against him could not boast of; in fact, they would rather no one mentioned their past records. With the stage set, George Weah ran for the Liberian presidency under the Congress for Democratic Change party (CDC).

The CDC party was the largest opposition party in the race. With Weah as the party standard, CDC quickly became a magnet for nearly the entire youth population of Liberia. Most of these young voters were weary of old politicians migrating from one party to another, recycling old promises that never came true for them. For those pessimistic voters, George Weah represented the change that they needed; in fact, most of them believed that he was the best-qualified candidate in the presidential race. Because Weah never supported any of the warring factions during the ugly Liberian civil wars, he could not be blamed for the problems that the country faced and was therefore lifted from the burden of answering questions regarding damage to the country's economy and infrastructure.

As the 2005 election day got underway, the Weah CDC party came first in the presidential polls, winning roughly 28.3% of the popular vote, but falling short of capturing the percentage required to avoid a runoff. Also vying for the presidency against him was Madam Ellen Johnson Sirleaf, a Harvard trained economist with a reservoir of domestic and international experience working for past Liberian administrations, the World Bank, and the United Nations, among other world organizations.

Mrs. Johnson Sirleaf was the standard of the Unity Party, UP, the second largest party in Liberia at the time. During the requisite runoff, political deal-making took place with much smaller political parties for their support. The argument made by the Unity Party during the runoff campaign was that although George Weah was the choice of youth voters, the grandmother in the race, Mrs. Ellen Johnson Sirleaf brought with her a sea wave of experience and international connection that was critically needed to rebuild a war-ravaged economy. Her supporters concluded that her education and experience in government, along with her international popularity was needed for Liberia to get back on its footing, not a popular president with no political or governmental experience.

Prior to Weah running for the presidency, he had no track record of working for the Liberian government, which was both a positive and a negative for him. This represented a challenge he needed to navigate carefully, especially when questions about his experience were raised. The positive for him was that no one could point fingers at him for supporting the destruction of the country or being corrupt—a common failure that almost every Liberian placed at the feet of past and present government officials. However, when the question regarding experience was brought up as a litmus test for the presidency, Weah often found himself sidelined from the discussion.

Weah's lack of political background coming into the race was a double-edged sword. As the campaign ended, he and his many supporters were losing the argument of who was best qualified to lead the country from its post-war status into a post-war democracy with economic sustainability. These were questioning that the Liberian people had to decide on leading into the November runoff election about selecting between two candidates who, by all accounts, would both make history for Liberia and the African continent. If elected, Mrs. Johnson Sirleaf would be the first female president and the African continent's first woman president and if Weah was the winner of the runoff and got elected, he would be the nation's second indigenous president after Samuel Doe. He would also be the nation's first soccer star and self-made millionaire to become president.

In November 2005, the stage was set for the runoff election between George Weah, the millionaire soccer superstar, and Mrs. Ellen Johnson Sirleaf, the Harvard-trained grandmother and World Bank economist to face each other. As the results of the polling poured in, Weah's poll numbers were counted at 40.6%, while Mrs. Sirleaf clocked a comfortable percentage of 59.4% of the votes, making her the clear winner of the 2005 presidential election in Liberia as the first female president of an African nation. For George Weah, who had always been on the winning side of things in his career, this was his first major setback. He, however, believed that loss was not the end of a man's life; he believed in standing up and brushing off the dust, ready to plan another strategy.

That is exactly what George did. He dusted himself off and began to prepare to take another shot at the presidency six years hence. His rival then was the same person who defeated him in the 2005 presidential election, the Liberian Iron Lady, President Ellen Johnson Sirleaf who was completing her first term and was up for reelection. George Weah saw a chance to challenge her on her six-year record of accomplishment, which for most Liberians was questionable and needed to be examined. As Mr. Weah expressed his interest in running for the second time, the same old question that had been hovering over him came back him again. This time the question was whether he was prepared enough the second time around to make his case to Liberians that he was now better qualified to replaced President Ellen Johnson Sirleaf. After launching his second bid to unseat his rival, he soon learned that the same questions about his qualifications unfortunately came back to haunt him again.

The impediment for Weah was that Liberians were beginning to see and feel the signs of improvement under President Sirleaf, and they were prepared to give her another chance. Under Mrs. Sirleaf, during her six-year tenure the Liberian people were growing more optimistic about the future of their beloved country, and they were not prepared to let it slide back to where it was before Mrs. Ellen Johnson Sirleaf took over. Under Mrs. Johnson, for the first time the media were experiencing an unrestrained amount of press freedom followed by other national and international accomplishments during her first term. She negotiated the national debt of $4.5 billion that was mostly piled up by past corrupt administrations before her. Meanwhile, in his quest to win the presidency the second time around in 2011, Weah selected a well-seasoned and prominent, popular Liberian politician as his running mate, hoping that his presence on his ticket would prevent voters from asking the questions about Weah's educational background and political experience again.

Most critics of the Weah/Tubman team believed that George Weah's selection of him was a way for Weah to divert the attention of Liberian voters away from him. Winston Tubman, George Weah's running mate, was the son of the former Liberian president William V.S. Tubman, who was once the longest-serving president and considered the father of modern Liberia. Winston, prior to his selection as Weah's running mate, had mostly stayed away from the Liberian political arena. A career diplomat and a prominent lawyer, he had lived most of his life in the U.S.A. Winston Tubman's experience certainly qualified him to absorb all the experience gaps that were weighing down the standard-bearer of the CDC party, Mr. George Weah.

However, despite Weah and Tubman's popularity and heavy showing during his second attempt at the executive mansion, Mrs. Johnson Sirleaf defeated him for the second time in the 2011 election. Although election results were covered by news of voting irregularities, the election was not by any means marred by the typical violence often seen in Africa after a major contested election. In the end, Weah and the CDC party graciously conceded defeat and accepted the 2011 election results. Mrs. Ellen Johnson Sirleaf was re-elected by the Liberian people for another six-year term.

Weah's second defeat did not diminish the support of his most admired supporters, Liberian youth. Nothing would make them relinquish their support for from him. However, their vote alone could not elect him to the office of the presidency. He would have to convince a large cross-section of the professional and intellectual population to help push him to the finish line. But first, he would have to convince the crossover and fence-sitters who were willing to go to any candidate who promised them what could not possibly be delivered. For some Weah had to address the issues surrounding his political experience and educational attainments before getting their vote. Following his second defeat, rather than give it all up and retreat to the comfort of his Miami mansion with his wife and children, Weah with his steel-like tenacity, made another attempt at the presidency for a third time.

However, before the third attempt, Weah underwent a self-evaluation and correction. His quest for the presidency has always been overshadowed by the question of experience and his lack of higher education. Though by now he had acquired a bachelor's degree, it was still not enough for some crossover politicians and other sections of disaffected professional groups to give him their votes. Meanwhile, the question about his love for the country and his unblemished record was never an issue that was brought up; in fact, it was one of his greatest assets coming into the Liberian political arena. George Weah knew that his chance at the presidency lay with him convincing the fence-sitters, so he immediately began by addressing the weak link that had prevented him from attaining highest office in the land.

Unfortunately for Weah, he spoke to the level where most ordinary Liberians could understand him. He spoke clearly for the youth to understand him without using elitist jargon that many Liberians would fail to understand. In a world of interpersonal communication, his ability to relay his message well to millions of ordinary Liberians should have served him well as a good communicator.

But his detractors used his ability to communicate with ordinary Liberians by branding his colloquial English as a weakness. It should be noted that Weah was clearly not a great orator with a strong command of the English language, but he could speak eloquently enough for ordinary citizens to understand. With the next election coming up in six-years, which would be bringing an end to

President Sirleaf's final term of governance, the field was clear for Weah to make his third attempt. Because the woman who defeated him twice was no longer in the race, he was now the candidate with the most formidable base of supporters.

First, however, he would have to address the two main issues that continued to cloud his chance at the highest office of the Liberian government. Meanwhile, taking a lesson from his respected successful and overachieving accomplishments, Weah returned to the United States to advance his education with a graduate degree. While in the United States at his home in Florida, he enrolled at an online university and earned a master's degree in public administration, finally ending the issue of his education.

In 2014 he returned to Liberia and threw his hat in the ring for the open senatorial position for Montserrado County. For Weah and his supporters, Montserrado County was going to be a great political test for him if he were to acquire the level of political experience needed for the presidency of Liberia. Montserrado County is where the capital Monrovia is located, the seat of the Liberian government. Montserrado is also the most populated and wealthy county in Liberia with the highest number of CDC voters, so a senatorial win for Weah would finally put to rest the question about his political experience in government.

As he jumped into the race for the senatorial seat for Montserrado County, many of his silent supporters and those still sitting on the fence along with disenfranchised professionals applauded his move and praised him for his political brilliance. Some mentioned that his decision to run for the senate was the best decision in his political career. If he won, no longer would his critics have anything to complain about, but first, he would have to defeat other heavyweights in the race, including one of the president's sons. As the race came to an end, Weah emerged as the clear and decisive winner. He won the Montserrado senatorial race by a wide margin, which marked a turning point in his political future. With a big political victory under his belt, he began serving in the Liberian Senate in December of 2014 and quickly began learning the art of politicking, deal-making, and passing legislation for the people of his district.

While serving as Montserrado County senator, Weah had his sights set on the 2017 election to replace President Ellen Johnson Sirleaf. With his educational and political concerns taken care of, Weah's CDC party merged with two other political parties, forming a coalition. Weah's CDC party was the leading coalition partner in the Liberian political race. Much to his advantage, George Weah was chosen as the standard-bearer of the CDC coalition parties.

The party also made a bold move by selecting the wife of former president and warlord Charles Taylor as Weah's running mate. At the time of her selection, Mrs. Jewel Howard Taylor was a senior senator for Bong County, a county that her formerly imprisoned husband captured and used as the capital for his rebel incursion. Bong County was an important place for the CDC coalition with its dense population and party supporters. Mrs. Taylor's presence on the CDC's ticket also relieved many female voters who had enjoyed stable leadership under Ellen Johnson Sirleaf and worried about the country falling back into all male-dominated rule, or the "old boys club." Weah's CDC coalition party joined in the 2017 race along with several other parties, making it impossible for any single party or candidate to clinch the 50% percent majority needed.

Representing the president's Unity Party was her vice president, Mr. Joseph Boakai, a two-term vice president under Johnson Sirleaf. Meanwhile, after the end of the first round of the 2017 voting on October 10, 2017, Weah's CDC coalition party acquired 38% of the total votes cast, while the president's ruling Unity Party led by Vice President Boakai clinched 29% of the vote, coming in second place to Weah's CDC coalition party. In the end, both parties fell short of the 50 plus majority needed to clinch the winning ticket, so a rerun was scheduled for December 26, 2017 between Weah's CDC coalition party and the ruling Unity Party of Vice President Boakai and Ellen Johnson Sirleaf.

Once the stage was set for the runoff between Weah's CDC coalition party and Boakai's Unity Party, behind the scenes politics were going on, with both parties vigorously encouraging smaller parties for their supporters. While it was true that Weah's CDC coalition party was favored to emerge victoriously, it was certainly not a done deal, because President Johnson Sirleaf had not yet come up to endorse her own ruling party candidate, Vice President Boakai. She was sitting on the fence, indecisive or perhaps making a political calculation. Or maybe she knew who she was going to endorse from the start but was engaged in political deal making. Whatever caused the delay in endorsing a candidate, the people wanted to know her choice and it was desperately needed.

As the run-up campaign picked up speed and the president stayed silent with her endorsement, rumors began to spread about her not supporting her vice president. However, in truth she was in negotiation with Weah's coalition about endorsing their candidate, the man she had beaten twice for the seat that she was about to hand over. Amid the sea of rumors, the president finally came forward and announced her decision, throwing a monkey wrench into her vice president's campaign. After endorsing George Weah, he was now heading for smooth sailing to the finish line. On December 26, 2017, Weah's CDC coalition party was declared the winner of the 2017 Liberian general election with a resounding victory over Vice President Joseph Boakai's Unity Party.

With the victory and the presidency in hand, Weah once again made history, adding to his streak of winning records which started from the little slum of Clara Town in the suburbs of Monrovia when he started playing soccer barefoot on dusty, unpaved fields under the stewardship of his grandmother. On January 22, 2018, George Manneh Weah took the oath of office as Liberia's 24th president. His inauguration marked the end of nearly 45 years of troublesome, sometimes violent transitions of power in Liberian history. This transitional process was smooth, peaceful and fair. One more exciting thing that came out of this election (unlike the 2005 and 2011 elections under the stewardship of the international community), this election was all hands-on deck, conducted and supervised by the Liberian National Election committee.

The Liberian people, and particularly Mrs. Johnson Sirleaf, must be hailed for making the process violent- and conflict-free, especially at a time when disputed elections were setting countries around the globe on fire, and chaos reigned. Meanwhile, after careful examination of George Weah's life and accomplishments, it can be argued that he is a gift to the Liberian people and a gift to the African continent. While Weah's first year in office has been marked by corruption allegations and abuse of power, I believe that Weah's upbringing and the example that he lives is a vivid portrayal of a man gifted with heart and compassion. He is described as a man with a strong love of country and people. I believe that in his quest to appease partisan loyalists, Weah has surrounded himself with individuals who do not have the nation's best interests at heart and are bent on continuing the destructives sport of corruption that has ravaged the entire continent and the people of Liberia over the course of many decades. There are stay opportunity for Weah to bring to the Liberian people the change they deserve and yarn for. President Weah has it in his nature to do the right thing and to win, he was born a winner not a loser. His is the youngest and most successful Liberian of my generation and because the youths of Liberia are counting on him, to deliver, it's my hope that the skills and tenacity that took him from the slum of Clara Town to the beautiful and prestigious cities of Europe, will be apply as he navigate his way into mastering his leadership skills.

CHAPTER 15

LIBERIA: THE ANCESTRAL HOME OF THE BLACK AMERICAN

In America, in spite of the passage in the Declaration of Independence, its most powerful and philosophical statement which reads, "We hold these truths to be self-evident that all men are created equal, that they are endowed by their creator with certain inalienable rights, that among these are life, liberty and the pursuit of happiness." For American Blacks, this statement was nothing but a myth. The adoption on July 4, 1776 of the Declaration of Independence did not acknowledge Blacks as human beings deserving to have the pursuit of happiness applied to them. Meanwhile, Blacks, Indians, slaves, and women were purposely omitted from this right drawn by the framers of the Declaration of Independence.

The Black Americans' existence as humans was ignored by the eloquent words of the Declaration of Independence; they were not considered equals to the white man, and they were certainly not involved in any decision to choose those who governed their affairs in the American colonies. In Africa, before being sold into slavery, Blacks lived in a communal society where everyone was looked after by the village and allowed to pursue their individual dreams. While their dreams may have been different from that of the white man's dreams, they each at least had a dream to pursue. However, as a result of the American Revolutionary war, the issues of Black American slaves proved more complex, as thousands of Blacks joined ranks with the British to fight against the independence desired by the American colonies. for their freedom.

More than four thousand Blacks from the North joined the armed revolutionaries. Black Americans knew that by fighting alongside the British, they would be working their way out of slavery and into freedom. Most of those Blacks were from the states of Maryland and Virginia and were still subjected to slave treatment. Though many Blacks bought their way out of slavery by fighting alongside the British, they were still shackled by discriminatory laws and prejudice from Southerners.

In the mix of the chaos and carnage of war, thousands of Blacks seized the opportunity to pursue their own freedom by jumping onto British Ships. At the end of the war, thousands who left on British ships in pursuit of freedom settled in England, Nova Scotia, the West Indies and in Africa. Not all the Blacks that fought alongside the British took the opportunity to flee for freedom in foreign lands. Many opted to stay in America as free slaves, while carefully evading the reach of their former slave masters. The revolution and the threat of the Southern cotton economy due to the rise of the industrial economy in the northern states led to the end of slavery in most southern states, but the process was painfully slow.

The American Revolution painfully shed some light on the plight of Black Americans who had been ignored for centuries by the white majority government of the United States. Avenues were created for American Blacks to start demanding their basic human rights to white elite society in the United States. Small self-educated groups of Black Americans from all over the south and the northern parts of the United States pointed to the passages in the Declaration of Independence to voice their concerns.

Many demanded that the U.S. Congress and its state legislatures end the savage and discriminatory business of slavery in America and finally give Black Americans equal rights that are guaranteed to all within the United States Constitution. As more Blacks joined ranks in demanding their freedoms, Blacks in other states began to demand their rights from local and state legislatures. Rights for Blacks had been denied them for decades but were freely and unquestionably provided to their white counterparts. In the state of Virginia, Blacks asked for the rights to testify in court against their fellow white citizens, a fundamental right that American Blacks had been denied in most southern and northern states.

In Nashville, Tennessee, for example, Blacks asked for the right to equal opportunity so they could have the ability to do well for themselves as individual members of society. In Massachusetts Blacks asked for the same financial assistance that the state gave to whites to educate their children and for training to learn current methods of mechanized farming. In other states, Black Americans asked for the repeal of discriminatory laws that were targeted at them.

Also, in Massachusetts, seven members of the Black American community voiced concern to the legislature about receiving the right to vote. They presented the argument that it was unjust to have a government that taxed them while the same government denied their right and privilege to vote. In their argument they wrote, "We apprehend ourselves to be aggrieved, in that while we are not allowed the privilege of freemen of the state, having no vote or influence in the election of those that tax us, yet many of us colored people have cheerfully entered the field of battle in the defense of the common cause and that as we conceive against a similar exertion of power regarding taxation too well known to need a recital in this place."

The demands for recognition of the rights of African Americans were a constant battle despite the constitutional guarantee of those rights. On the other hand, self-educated Black Americans did not relent in their push for the total abolishment of slavery, discriminatory laws and the recognition of equal rights for Blacks everywhere in America. One of those self-educated Blacks leading the charge was Benjamin Banneker, a Black man, who taught himself mathematics and astronomy. He accurately predicted a solar eclipse and was appointed to work on the planning of the new city of Washington. Banneker wrote to Thomas Jefferson, "I suppose it is a truth too well attested to you to need a proof here, that we are a race of beings who have long labored under the abuse and censure of the world; that we have long been looked upon with eyes of contempt; and that we have been long considered rather as brutish than human, and scarcely capable of mental endowments .. I apprehend you will embrace every opportunity to eradicate that train of absurd and false ideas and opinions which so generally prevail concerning us; and that your sentiments are concurrent with mine, which are that one universal father hath given being to us all; and that he hath not also, without partiality, afforded us all with the same sensations and endowed us all with the same faculties."

Benjamin added his voice to those of many other self-educated slaves who relentlessly inundated the white elitist society to grant the constitutional guarantee in the Declaration passage, "That ALL Men Were Created Equal." In his letter, he rebuked Jefferson to relieve himself of those prejudices that had sponged his thoughts since he had continued to retain Blacks in America. However, despite the effort of Banneker and other self-educated and bold spoken Blacks whose messages were directed at powerful white society, not much was done to enhance their conditions in America. Banneker's letter might have persuaded Jefferson to a degree as he went out of his way to educate the elite ruling white class about the conditions of American's Black population.

Fundamental American culture, the economic benefit of the slave trade, the power of the southern plantation owners and the growing business interests between the political elite from southern and northern states made it harder to advance the causes of America's Black minority significantly. Also impeding the progress for Black equal rights in America was the centuries-old racial hatred and prejudice that had long intoxicated the American colonies. Jefferson's own inability to relinquish himself of slaves as property, caused him to fail to live up to his own philosophical views, and he remained a slave owner until his death. Despite concerted efforts to advance the rights of Black Americans in pre-revolutionary America, their status as an inferior class, along with native Indians from post-revolutionary American society, was never settled in the American colonies until the end of the Civil War.

Once the British were no longer a threat to the newly independent American colonies, white elites were unrestrained in putting their ideas on paper of an America they envisioned to be theirs and theirs only. The white ruling class wanted to solidify their elitist status as the sole beneficiaries of post-revolutionary American society. To legitimize their racist ideas, they met in Philadelphia at a convention to draft the new United States Constitution. Leaders from the Revolutionary War met in 1787 to draft the document that led to the birth of the U.S. Constitution. Their efforts were viewed by many at that time and even now as the brilliant work of wise men whose ingenuity created a proposed framework for the world's greatest democracy.

However, what the document lacked at the time and even now is the guarantee of equal rights for all Americans. Some historians have reviewed the work and true intent of the drafters of the United States constitution and most question what the true intent of the drafters was when they mentioned equality. Did they mean equality for all, or for the rich and powerful white men?

Historian Charles Beard opened the minds of many historians when he wrote about the economic interpretation of the Constitution of the United States. He said that the rich (meaning the white ruling class) must in their own interest either control the government directly or control the laws by which the government operates. Beard verified his theory by examining the construct of the U.S. Constitution in which he presented the economic backgrounds and political views of the fifty-five men who assembled in the city of Philadelphia in 1787 to draft the Constitution.

Beard writes of his study of the drafters that most of the participants were men of various professional backgrounds, some were lawyers, wealthy businessmen, rich farmers. Some were rich from the forceful accumulation and seizure of Indian lands, and some were holders of Black people as property. Others were in the manufacturing and shipping industries. Some of them were money loaners for interest, and government bondholders. Forty of the fifty-five men, according to Treasury Department records, had some direct economic interest in establishing a strong federal government that protected their interests. Among the drafters, the money lenders wanted to abolish the use of paper money to pay off debts, land speculators wanted protection as they forcefully amassed Indian lands; the bondholders wanted a government that was capable of raising money by imposing nationwide taxation on the citizens to pay off bonds. On the other hand, slave owners wanted federal security against Black slave revolts and runaways, and men who were manufacturers needed tariff protection. Charles Beard acknowledged that he does not believe that the drafters of the U.S. Constitution wrote the document only to enrich themselves, but he cautions readers not to ignore the fortunes and business interests of many of the founding fathers.

It is worth noting that constitutional limitations on voting severely held back American Blacks, American Indians and women, as in many states the right to vote was provided only to property owners. As a result, America's post-revolutionary democracy only benefited rich and influential white elite groups. Two groups eventually emerged: Federalists, who supported the current constitution and anti-Federalists, opponents of the constitutional unity. For purposes of keeping unity between the thirteen original states and the slave commercial interests of the south and the northern manufacturing commercial interests, a constitutional compromise was reached between both interest groups. For the commercial interests of the north, delegates requested laws that would regulate interstate commerce and demanded that such laws require only most of the Congress to enact.

Southerners were in no hurry to end the commerce of slavery since their wealth accumulation and influence depended on slave trading. Consequently, southerners agreed to the northerners' demands in return for allowing the commercial slave trading to continue for nearly two more decades before finally being outlawed. Therefore, for at least twenty more years, the plight of Blacks in America continued to be invisible to the white wealthy class. The United States government relinquished its moral and legal responsibility to protect the rights of its Black citizens, many of whom were still held in bondage and treated inhumanely by racists and wealthy white plantation owners. Readers here need to know that one of the sole purposes of the United States government's support of the slave trade was based strictly on economic practicality.

By 1790, the south was producing thousands of tons of cotton every year. This number later increased by hundreds of thousands of tons of cotton by 1860. This meant that more slaves were needed to meet the cotton demand. With five hundred thousand slaves already in the United States, that number quickly grew to four million slaves as the U.S. managed the most successful system designed by white capitalists as an instrument for wealth building, a system they were not persuaded to forego.

It would require numerous slave revolts and a full-scale civil war to untangle the deeply entrenched American slavery system. As predicted, large scale violence that led to the American Civil War, along with the courageous actions of freed Black slaves in concert with white abolitionists from the north to end the ugly slave trade in America. By 1808 the United States government made it illegal to import slaves into the American colonies. However, it would take several more decades for the law to be fully enforced by the U.S. government. According to historian John Hope Franklin in his book titled, *From Slavery to Freedom,* "The long-unprotected coast, the certain markets and the prospects of huge profits were too much for the American merchants and they yielded to the temptation." Franklin estimated that perhaps nearly 250,000 slaves were imported into the United States after the law was passed that abolished the slave trade.

As more flamboyant politicians, including abolitionists opposed slavery in America, many still could not see Blacks as equals, so they reiterated the constant theme of sending Blacks back to Africa as the only solution. Meanwhile, many abolitionists, both Black and white, along with some wealthy northern businessmen in America adopted the notion that it was impossible for the two races to peacefully integrate into American society, so they supported the idea of an African American colony in Africa. As the tide of opinion against slavery in America was gaining steam, the American colonization society was founded in 1816 and began the process of resettling freed Black Americans in what is now Liberia. The first freed Black American slaves landed in Liberia in 1822. Shortly after that, Jehudi Ashmun, a white American, arrived in the new colony and began the formation of the new government and laws of Liberia.

Before the formation of Liberia during the 1810s and 1820s, there had been resettlement attempts of African Americans back to Africa, most of which were unsuccessful. The creation of Liberia was one of the remarkable success stories and achievements of black Americans. It marked the most notable attempt made by nearly 6,000 freed Black American slaves to escape racial persecution in the United States to form a colony of their own on another continent.

Meanwhile, successful ventures were not as easy since they faced several adverse difficulties at the embryonic stages of the creation of Liberia. The American Society for the Colonization of Free People of Color from the United States and the American Colonization Society were the principal sponsors of the creation of the new Liberian nation. These societies eventually faced financial challenges and could no longer provide monetary support to the new colony in Africa. Other challenges the new nation faced were the constant threats from the native populations, who had reservations about the settlement of freed Black Americans slaves on their land. Also challenging for the new Black American settlers were the constant bloody skirmishes between the settlers and the native populations, along with famine and diseases which made it harder to grow the fledgling population of new settlers. Back in America, news of settlers dying of disease and in bloody skirmishes made it harder for other freed Black slaves to embark on the journey to the new Liberian colony.

As a result of the American government's refusal to pledge adequate defense and financial support for the settlers, Liberia was forced to declare its independence in 1847 out of fear of being invaded by the powerful British navy stationed nearby. Joseph Jenkins Roberts, born a freedman in the United States and one of whose grandparents were Black, became the first president of Liberia and a constitution was established along the lines of the United States constitution. It was not until the mid-1840s and 1850s that the settlement's population saw a dramatic increase as mass migration to the new republic began. By the 1860s and on into the 1900's several thousand Black American freedmen and women migrated to Liberia from America and settled. Other arrivals came from central, north, south and east African countries to resettle in Liberia, as it was the only free Black republic existing at the time. Additionally, for the love of liberty and freedom, many Black Americans relocated to Liberia. Other reasons that Black migration took place was due to the withdrawal of federal troop positions in U.S. southern states, put in place to protect Blacks and to enforce federal laws that southern states willfully ignored.

It must be noted that Liberia was an experiment in thought. At the time, most whites and including some Blacks believed that the Black race was inferior to whites and its people were incapable of managing their affairs without being overseen by white masters. Some accepted the notion that slavery was the best thing that ever happened to Blacks. They erroneously claimed that slavery was an opportunity for Blacks to excel in civilization. So, the idea of a Black owned republic was not logical for these doubters of Black capabilities. Some argued that Blacks were unable to govern by themselves. Many of these white doubters of Black intelligence had never seen Black people control anything of their own before, so you can imagine where their pessimistic views originated from. Black slaves in America had always depended on their masters for their considerably basic needs such as food, clothing and a place to sleep which was usually the bare minimum to meet the needs of the growing number of slaves. So, the notion of governing themselves in a faraway continent without the white master's control was unimaginable at the time by many of these doubters.

Because of slavery many Black Americans had never been led or governed by another Black person. All they knew at the time was turning to their masters for any mundane matter concerning their affairs. For these Black slaves, when the slave master said yes it was yes, and when he said no it was no, end of story. It was not that Blacks were inferior to whites due to genetic differences or dispositions, as some prejudiced and ignorant whites would have you believe. Black slaves at the time felt inferior to their white masters, not because of their intelligent dispositions, but rather because of the racial subjugations that were placed upon them.

Meanwhile, as the crusade for the return to Africa was gathering steam, not every Black seized on the notion to migrate to Liberia. Instead of allowing the ACS to resettle them in a faraway land, they contended under no uncertain terms that their birthplace was America, where their fathers fought, bled and died, and they would not be deported to different soil. A Baptist preacher named Nathaniel Paul who was resistant to the relocation to Africa, wrote to the ACS telling them, "You may go ahead with your plan to deport this element to make slavery secure," he warned, "But the free negroes will never emigrate to Africa. We shall stay here and fight until the foul monster is crushed. Slavery must go!" he declared.

You can see that not every free Black American was on board to migrate to Liberia for a chance to govern himself. Since many were born in the United States of America, just as their forebears had, they were in no hurry to abandon it for a place they had no close connections to or memories of. Those who yielded to the call to migrate to Liberia felt the weight and challenges of establishing a state and government run by Blacks, first of its kind in pre-modern times. With a government in place and independence declared, Liberia began the process of building a modern democracy headed by freed Black Americans, a people once told that they were incapable of governing their own affairs.

In the 1800s, during the early formation of Liberia, democracy it was not perfect, simply put. It did not include all inhabitants; natives were excluded from the document that established the republic of Liberia. Neither was the American democracy anywhere near perfect; it did not include all its inhabitants as well. For example, Blacks, women, and native Indians were excluded from nearly every decision of the affairs that governed them. It would take several decades before American minority groups and women would have any role in deciding the affairs of their government.

In the Black American colony of Liberia, women could vote decades before America would follow its footsteps. In addition, elsewhere in the European continent, democratic governments were nowhere in sight. For example, although far away from Liberia, Europe's first known modern democracy was declared in France, but it soon descended into anarchy.

In 1848, one year after free Black slaves from America declared Liberia as an independent nation, France, made another attempt at democracy, but within a year Louis Napoleon Bonaparte seized power and began dismantling the democratic system in France. Fortunately for the French people, his regime of terror collapsed in 1870. France's attempts at building a vibrant democratic society would take several more decades to achieve. France needed five trials to finally get it right, which occurred after the end of the Algerian war in 1958 when Charles De Gaulle ascended to the presidency.

At the same time, other countries were also struggling to build democratic governments. In Italy, for example, democracy did not come to realization until after World War II. This occurred after a disruptive period of fascism. Also, on the path toward democracy was Germany. It did emerge from its dictatorship, eventually becoming a liberal democracy, but not until after WWII. Also, in Europe, Spain had a long tumultuous struggle on its path toward democracy. Spain travelled through a major crisis that included civil wars, military interventions, and dictatorships.

However, a more sustainable and durable democracy came for Spain in the mid-1970s. As you can see by the history of these powerful western countries ruled by the white race, most struggled immensely with the ability to govern themselves. Their successful systems of democracy rarely came easily. Success was accomplished through trial and failure, as is always the case in building a vibrant democracy. So, the idea that Blacks are incapable of governing themselves within a democratic system is fully based on ignorance, prejudice, propaganda, and is not supported by fact.

If Liberia were to fail at democracy after its establishment, it would have been because the institution of slavery had indoctrinated the psyches and minds of the free Blacks who established the first modern democracy in Africa's oldest republic. Liberia's democracy failed, not because its citizens were Black and biologically incapable of controlling their own affairs. The lesson of all world democracies in history is that successful democracies rarely come easily or smoothly, and neither do they come quickly.

Regardless of race and culture, the lessons of history have revealed and are still revealing to the world that the road to a true and sustainable democracy is long, narrow, rough, and sometimes bloody. Liberia's path toward the building of its democracy in the 1800s was at least believed to be successful despite the exclusion of the indigenous population from affairs of government, which observers argue was due to the slavery mentality inflicted on the free Black American founders by white U.S. slave owners that was carried back to the African continent and imposed on native Liberians.

As Liberia was experiencing democracy, many European countries were struggling with building their own systems of democracy. On the African continent, when many countries in sub-Saharan Africa were under the dominance of colonial rules, Liberians boasted of freedom and democracy. Liberia was also in the forefront fighting against the dominance of colonial oppression and apartheid in South Africa. At the time when many leaders that were at the forefront of African freedom and the untangling of Africa from the colonial white regimes, some sought refuge and support in Liberia. Not only did Liberia gave refuge to African liberators, but support was also given for the liberation of Europe from Nazi Germany. Liberia supported the allies both in WWI and again in WWII. Liberia was also among the countries that championed the establishment of the League of Nations, now known as the United Nations.

On the African front, Liberia also joined ranks with Dr. Kwame Nkrumah and President Sekou Toure for the promotion of African unity and a united Africa. All these accomplishments are things to look back upon and reflect how far we have traveled on the difficult road of building a sustainable and prudent democracy. In Liberia, there is no disagreement that the nation's democratic institutions are not without problems. But when you look around the world, you can honestly admit that currently there is no known democracy, old or new, that is without problems.

For example, some nations that were once considered beacons of hope for the sustainability of democracy, are falling back in the past to a time when the idea of democracy was looked down upon. Even 21st century America still struggles with the issues of its minority populations' rights. Incidences of voter suppression still prevail in many southern states and occasionally in some northern states. In Europe and the Middle East, marginalized groups are being prosecuted, segregated and economically disenfranchised by the ruling elite and the corporate ruling class. Many are being persecuted and marginalized because of their religion, race or cultural origins.

The once cherished institution of democracy has vehemently been challenged by the sea waves of nationalistic ideologies that are unveiling around European countries and elsewhere, including Donald Trump's America. With all of these uncertainties about the future of modern democracy around the world, including my adopted country the United States, now it is the time for tenacious Black Americans, Americo Liberians, and the indigenous Liberians to strongly join forces and work hard in making the dreams of a free land of liberty, freedom, and democracy in Liberia a reality for the Black race and the African continent as a whole.

Understanding that the only reason Liberia became a nation is that Blacks were sold into slavery after hundreds of years of persecution and racial discrimination, marginalization, exploitation and inhumane treatment at the hands of their white slave owners. They decided that the only way to escape the white men's racial persecution and torture was to return to their ancestors' land to accomplish that long-held viewed, Liberia was established as a land for the free Black Americans to settle.

Unfortunately, however, the history of Liberia is not known by today's generation of Black Americans. It saddens me to say that there has not been adequate effort made by historians, politicians and influential personalities from both sides in making the case for Black Americans to reconnect with their ancestral land, Liberia. While there is no denying that most Black Americans acknowledge that their ancestors came from Africa, most lack the awareness that most of their ancestors returned to Africa at a critical time in the history of the Black American adventures and settled in Liberia. These historical facts are important for the new generation of Black Americans or Americo Liberians to know, especially at a time where nationalism is at the forefront of nearly every political and social debate.

In America, almost every ethnic group identifies with one country or another as their ancestral homeland. The Italian Americans will tell you they are proud that they are Italian Americans and speak a type of broken Italian to prove their connection. Mexican Americans, on the other hand, are also proud to let you know in their deep accents that they are Mexican Americans, despite the occasional prejudices that they face, especially in Trump's America. Additionally, Irish, Polish, Germany, and Israeli Americans are proud to identify with their ancestral homelands and you barely hear them refer to themselves as European Americans. Most white Americans would rather point to the country in Europe that their parents, parents came from or settled in. It would be nice if Black Americans attached themselves to Liberia and referred to themselves as Americo Liberians, because that is what their ancestors, the founders of Liberia, were called.

While it is true that Black American ancestors came from Africa, it is also true that the Africans sold into slavery did not come from all over the African continent. The slave trades were concentrated in the coastal area of sub-Saharan Africa, which includes present-day Liberia, Sierra Leone, Gambia, Senegal, Ghana, Congo and other areas of the west coasts. However, what is known as fact is that when the slaves returned to Africa as freedmen, they settled in Liberia and made it a republic of their own, something every generation of Black Americans should be proud of and stay connected with. I would argue that Black Americans should stay connected with Liberia just as the Jews, and European Americans stay connected with their ancestral homeland. There are so many cultural similarities that if the current generation were to travel to Liberia, they would easily find themselves submerged into the Liberian cultural fabric without knowing that they were far away from the American shore of the inner cities and downtowns.

A Black American friend once told me that he made a conscious decision to travel to Ghana after reading some historical information about where his slave ancestors might have come from. While in Ghana he said that for the first time in his life he understood and experienced what it feels like to belong to the majority race in a country. Africa is predominantly Black, but he was still able to get a feeling of being a member of the majority population for the first time.

"Everywhere I went while in Accra, I saw people that looked like someone in my family back in America. In a shopping center in downtown Accra, I nearly ran into a woman who looks just like my uncle's ex-wife. When I saw her, I stared, wondering what she was doing in Africa. But soon I overheard her speaking to another lady in a very deep Ghanaian English accent, I immediately stopped in my tracks." My friend has since visited Ghana and other parts of Africa every year now with his own wife and kids. He described their experience as breathtaking. He said rather than going to Mexico, Europe and the Caribbean Islands he preferred going to Africa for his vacations. "The continent is amazingly beautiful," he said.

The excitement in his demeanor represented a man who was once felt lost but rediscovered himself by tracing his roots. However, I have met Black Americans, some educated and some not very educated, that have asked some of the most stupid questions and stored some of the most racist and prejudiced views of Africa than many of my white American friends. For example, a Black American friend and a co-worker once asked me if I used to sleep in trees back in Africa. I was flabbergasted and somehow insulted, and worse, angered by his useless question, especially coming from a Black man. Meanwhile, before I could respond to his stupid question, one of my white co-workers who had traveled to Africa on many occasions interrupted and said, "Dude, are you stupid"? Nobody sleeps in trees in Africa. I have traveled twice to Morocco, Nigeria and Egypt, and many of the places look like many of our cities and towns. "Dude, you need to get out of Trenton and go see the world," he angrily rebuked our African American co-worker. My anger for my Black American friend quickly turned into an awkward moment as he realized the blunder he had just made.

On another occasion, one of my Black American friends told me that he would never go to Africa because he might get eaten by lions or wild animals. My response to him was that you stand a better chance of being eaten by a lion or wild animal in the streets of New York and Philadelphia than in the capital cities of any African country. He looked at me like I had seven horns and was perhaps losing my mind. This guy lacked basic facts of history and awareness of his own culture. For most historical recordings, Black Americans have been purposely miseducated about their race, culture, and about Africa in general. They have been made to believe that Africa has nothing to contribute to the world and that it is a "godforsaken continent." As a result, some Black Americans are embarrassed to be connected to Africa, and some are even embarrassed to be called African American. They would rather be called "nigger" than be called African or African American. Some of these lampooned individuals have taken an overly large dose of the white men's medicine and cannot help themselves.

Meanwhile during my research in preparing to write this book, I came upon many instances of ignorance of Blacks about their own cultural denial about Africa and anything associated with its greatness. I no longer fault the many ignorant Blacks who through no fault of their own have been poorly educated and robbed of their own independent to decipher facts from fictions about Africa. This, of course, is designed to keep Black Americans separated from the continent of their Black ancestors and its riches.

It grieved me to look at all the many beautiful tourist destinations and pristine beaches of Africa crowded by Caucasians who are enjoying the natural beauty of the land. When you look around you, you hardly see African Americans anywhere around you. White Europeans come from all over Europe to experience the natural wildlife and intricate, diverse beautiful cultures of Africa. Some own properties, making money off other Europeans who are traveling there for vacations. I would love to see Black Americans owning properties and having travel destinations in Liberia and other parts of Africa before it's all taken over by white Europeans that have been ravaging the continent for centuries with guns that fuel conflict and steal the continent's natural resources.

After the Europeans, the Chinese are now rolling into Africa in sea waves, enjoying the beauty and growing economic picture of Africa. For many Black Americans, the closest they have ever come to Africa is going to Jamaica or some Caribbean island. As Africa is poised to become one of the faster growing economies in the world and the location of resources for the protection of our beautiful climate, the economic empowerment of its people is now more critical than ever before. It will do Africa no good if its vibrant young generations are not educationally and technologically prepared to meet the challenges of a future uniquely positioned to be their own.

The rest of humanity is closely watching Africa. The white European race has continuously sucked the revenue out of Africa for centuries, right up to this date, they continue to do so. Sadly, the Chinese are coming to join the party by providing useless projects to corrupt governments and placing those countries in the stranglehold of debt and poverty just like the Europeans and the Americans did to many parts of Africa. Africa today is held back because of those corrupt debts incurred by past leaders who were puppets for their white masters' and sponsors' governments. This is my cry to all Black Americans,

Americo Liberians and the indigenous Liberians. There are many sinister reasons behind why contemporary white historians have purposely distorted the importance of African history and culture, perhaps by design or willful ignorance of our history, which has led to an unnecessary and purposely limited understanding of our historical past. This lack of understanding is inadvertently affecting our understanding of what our future history should be.

In a world of purposeful misinformation, fake news, political dissent, vague competing voices and technology that are purposely manipulated to stoke biases to determine a particular outcome on social media, it is now more important than ever before to grasp a understanding of our history and how it shapes our views of the world that we live in. Additionally, strides in technology and communications are bringing our isolated corners and stellar spaces into orbiting proximity. As a result, our togetherness as members of the same human family, and the principle of universal peace, rule of law and economic prosperity are drawn closer than before. As Black people, especially Africans, we must stop taking the western depiction of our history at face value. We can no longer allow the prejudiced western opinions of our people to be our opinions of ourselves, but rather we should vigorously be the narrators and salespeople of our own culture, customs, and history.

EPILOGUE

For far too long the historical depiction of the Black race has somehow predominantly been written by Western historians, who for various reasons and sometimes out of willful ignorance and prejudice. These misguided writers for centuries have portrayed the white race as the inventors and enablers of civilization, while they glaringly portrayed the Black race as savages who contributed nothing to humanity other than backward ideas. These so-called contemporary western historians went out of their way to justify slavery as necessary in order to bring the savage Blacks to their so-called civilized ways of life. This book is not a rebuke against the white race for what they did to Black Africans who were captured and sold into slavery in the Americas and Europe.

The main reason for writing this book has to do with my love for history, culture and customs of people of the world. I certainly subscribe to the belief that if you do not understand where you are coming from, you certainly will not know where you are going. Though I do not refer to myself as an historian, I certainly describe myself as an inquisitive reader of political history and customs of people in the same universe. Recently I derived eminent pleasure from learning the cultural, social, and political connections of the people of Liberia and the people of the United States. I am profoundly tied to both countries in unique ways that have inspired me to dig deeper into the history of these two countries and their people.

Liberia, which is my country of birth, and the United States, which is my country of naturalization and the birth country of my children, has contributed immensely to the person I am today. I am profoundly grateful for the opportunity that my adopted country provided me. I could never trade my love and patriotism for any other places in the world except the United States and the Republic of Liberia. With that said, the sole purpose for writing this book is to provide a chronological account of the true nature of Liberia's and the USA's rich cultural, social, political and historical similarities. Many parallels exist between Liberians and the American Blacks, Americo Liberians, and the often-ignored indigenous Liberian people.

My hope for this publication is to shine light on the evolution of Liberia's birth. In a time of economic deprivation of Blacks in the United States, there were those who believed that America's race problem would only end if American Blacks were deported back to Africa, a land that many had no connection with at all. It was at this juncture that the idea of a Black-owned land and sovereignty was conceived and later birthed as a small colony which later became known as Liberia, or the Land of Liberty. Even though Liberia was established by the United States of America for the purpose of resettling its Black population, Liberia later became a place of migration for other Blacks and people of color fleeing oppression, racism, economic and political slavery from different parts of Africa and the Caribbean Islands.

Liberia became a melting pot and an example of a Black free land and modern democracy. Liberia, for its part during the Antebellum upheaval in the world, was enjoying democracy at a time when most eastern and western parts of Europe were practicing fascism and communism. In the United States, the country that gave birth to Liberia, was struggling to create a wholesome society that included all its citizens. These connections are particularly important for our Generation X to know and appreciate the history and struggle of past generations. If current generations understand the historical struggles of past generations, it will help provide a broader view of the paths they took for us to enjoy the numerous successes we have today.

My aim is to invigorate the fighting spirit of our ancestors that connects both the Black American experience, the Americo Liberian and the indigenous Liberians. With this aspirational quest, together we can foster the growth of the deep family and ancestral ties that connect our people. In the age of technology, with an overabundance of communication, media and social mobility, we can no longer excuse or wax nostalgic about learning, appreciating, and connecting with our own histories. As you conclude this book, my hope is for all our people to create intercultural and inter-educational awareness between our institutions of learning, thereby encouraging cultural awareness and tourism between Black Americans, Americo Liberians, and the indigenous Liberians. By strengthening these contacts, both groups would undoubtedly be on the paths to demystifying ages old cultural myths designed by colonial powers that have divided our people and kept them ignorant for far too long.

MY RECOMMENDATION

If indigenous Liberians, Americo Liberians and Black Americans are to reclaim their positions as strong contributor to global peace and democratic institutions, we must begin to act now. Now is the time for Liberians and Black Americans to dust off the decades-old slumber and quit reluctant observer role of their own history to become the sole narrators and salesmen of their global contribution to civilization, democracy, trade and technology. I am not suggesting here that Black Americans and their brothers and sisters in Liberia should ignore the contribution of other races in America and the world—that would be unwise and foolish.

What I am suggesting is that Black Americans are uniquely blessed to have connections to both continents and cultures. As the result of slavery, Black Americans have unfettered ownership to the history of America, due to the fact that since they were removed from the African continent and sold into slavery, they equally hold unfettered ownership to the history of Africa and Liberia. By nature of these facts, Black Americans should hold on to their American history but should always embrace their African history and progress.

Black Americans should not neglect the achievements of the African people, particularly from Liberia. We are quick to accept as fact the historical accounts of Rome, France, Greece or the United States and other places of the world, but when it comes to the history of the brilliant achievements of the free Black American men of color who navigated the ocean and established Africa's first modern republic and democracy, we give that less attention. For too long the Black race has focused too much on what other races developed and accomplished and have been careless or nit-picked about our own accomplishments.

We should now begin the process of focusing more on the things that we as Black people and Africans have developed and contributed to the world and start the process of advancing our own narratives. The influence of Songhay, Mali, Ethiopia, Ancient Ghana, Liberia and the small nation of Bennie should not be ignored anymore, especially not by Black people. When we mention the contributions of George Washington, Thomas Jefferson or Shakespeare, we should equally mention the accomplishments of Joseph Jerking Roberts, the first president of Africa's first republic. We should also mention William V.S. Tubman, who, along with Roberts, hold historical ties with the United States. We as Black people and Africans should not forget the gallantry of the many silent voices of Black Americans, as well as the many who give up their lives in the establishment of the United States and the Republic of Liberia. Together as people, for far too long we have focused on what other races have accomplished, and now we must take a turn toward our own people. We need to focus more on the things that the Black race has developed and contributed to our global ecosystem and take pride in it.

It is time for the Black American community to treat Liberia just as the Jews in Europe and around the world have treated Israel, not in a religious sense, but rather as the ancestral home of the Jewish people. Now that we have established the historical connection between Black Americans and their Liberian brothers and sisters, we should now draw our attention to some of the steps we need to take to foster the bond between the two cultures and peoples that are interwoven and inextricably intertwined, to say the least.

1. I believe that it is time for the Liberian government to open the door and encourage African Americans to come to their ancestors' land. Liberia.

2. The current Liberian government should promote and encourage Black American land ownership and business ownership in Liberia. This should be based on the Joseph Project, which in 2007, its 50th year of independence, initiated the Joseph Project to commemorate 200 years since the abolition of slavery and encourage Africans abroad to come home. Like Israel's policy of reaching out to Jews across Europe and beyond following the Holocaust, the Joseph Project is named for the Biblical Joseph who was sold into slavery in Egypt only to later reunite with his family and rule Egypt.

3. My hope is for the Liberian government to begin a program that will lead to issuing residency status to Black Americans who are willing to resettle in Liberia. This process should be fruitful after 2 to 3 years of residency in the country. For those who are willing to invest heavily in the country, their process to obtaining residency status should be expedited. Those who meet the residency requirements should be given a Black Card

like the Green Card issued by the United States government to foreign residents. After being a resident for four years, these new residents should automatically become citizens with certain restrictions, such as the ability to become president, vice president, speakers or chief justices of Liberia. The children of these new residents, however, that are born in Liberia, can run for the office of the presidency as outlined in the Liberian constitution.

4. In addition to fostering Black American and Liberian brotherhood, the Liberian government, along with historically Black colleges and universities should initiate the establishment of reciprocal relationships and understanding between the two peoples through educational institutions, churches and religious institutions as a way of fostering intellectual connections between the two people and cultures.

5. Black Americans must begin the process of establishing strong, powerful lobbying groups in Washington DC and on Capitol Hill that would begin to advocate for the security, democracy and economic empowerment of Liberia and the Liberian people, just like the powerful Jewish lobbying groups that connect with congressmen inside the hallways of the Capitol and White House, making sure that the needs of Israel are secure. In addition, I would like to see prominent African American voices, including politicians, business executives, celebrities, athletes and social influencers adding their voices to the dialogue that is geared toward reconnecting Black American to their ancestral land of Liberia.

6. The Liberian government and non-profit groups should create youth internships and cultural educational exchange programs between African American youth and their Liberian counterparts, beginning with middle- and high schoolers. None of these proposals are possible if we, together as a people do not strengthen our laws and engage all our citizens in the democratic process. Liberians must seriously and honestly shackle and strangle what I called the two Cs or African death traps that are robbing the people of their dignity and opportunity for a better chance in life and progress in the human world.

The two Cs are corruption and conflict. In many parts of Africa, including our beloved land of Liberia, corruption has become a national sport, where corrupt officials are rewarded with more government jobs and contracts so long, they help keep the people ignorant. Unfortunately for those affected people, they are conned into believing that those stealing government funds are smart and clever and should be respected. Conflict, on the other hand, can become an instrument to start divisions among people by corrupt tyrants and misguided leaders who strive and thrive on maintaining those divisions among people. When citizens are at loggerheads with each other, these misguided and corrupt leaders steals the resources of their people and siphoned it into their foreign banks accounts where it is used to develop the economy of the West, leaving the affected countries in Africa and people in poverty, underdeveloped and disease.

Finally, to properly engage all its citizens, Liberia needs an initiative for her local language to develop written forms that allow and encourage local dialect speakers to become literate in their history and laws. I am aware that it would be difficult to have every Liberian citizen speaking English which was adopted as the official language at the founding of the republic. However, what is achievable is the ability to develop written forms of each local dialect that can be transcribed into the official English language of Liberia. This would also allow the language to be transcribed into various dialects which would facilitate the people's understanding of their official government communications that are currently printed only in English.

Liberia has it within itself to be a pioneer in building a model for the subregion of Africa. The official language deficiency is not unique to Liberia; it is an ages old African problem that has its root cause in past colonial takeovers that led to many African countries adopting the languages of their colonial masters. Enriching and preserving the language diversity of Liberia demonstrates the importance of civics that engages and empowers citizens in modern participatory democracy. I look forward to the opportunity to be engaged in this process which is dear to my heart.

God Bless Liberia and God Bless the United States of America.

BIBLIOGRAPHY

Selected books and Pamphlets

Akingbade Harrison. "U.S.- Liberian Relations during World War II," Clark Atlanta University. Vol. 46, No.1,1ˢᵗ Qtr.,1985 pp.25-37.

Aptherker, Herbert. American Negro Slave Revolt, New York: International Publishers, 1963.

American Colonization Society. http://webby.cc.dension.edu//-waite/liberia/ history/acs.htm

___. (1967). A Biography of President William V.S Tubman. London, England

Boachen, A.Adu. Topics in West Africa. (Longmans, Green, CO Ltd, London, and Harlow.1969) Liberian History

Beard, J.R (John Relly), 1800-1876 Toussaint L'Ouverture; A Biography and Autobiography: 372 p;2iII. Publisher,221 Washington Street.1863.

Charles Hartung, 'Peacekeeping in Liberia: ECOMOG and the struggle for Order; Liberian Study Journal, Volume XXX, No.2, 2005

Dimsdale, Thomas J. The Vigilantes of Montana: or Popular Justice in the Rock Mountains, Third ed. Butte., Montana, W.F. Bartlett, 1915.

Dunn, Elwood D. Liberia, and the United States During the Cold War: Limits of Reciprocity, Palgrave Macmillan, New York, NY 2009.

Fred Van derKraaij,'The Open-Door Policy of Liberia- An Economic History of Modern Liberia' (Bremen, 1983,2 volumes) pp.1-5

February 06, 1820: FREED U.S. SLAVES DEPART ON JOURNEY TO AFRICA
URL
https:// www.history.com/this-day-in-history/freed-U.S.slaves-depart-on-journey-to-africa
Accessed on July 04, 2018- publisher, A+Networks.

From Slavery to Freedom: The African- American Pamphlet Collection, 1822-1909 Collection Connections/ Teacher Resources Library of Congress/teachers/ classroommaterials/connections/slavery/file.htm) Retrieved on 11/14/2019.

Johnston, Sir Harry. Liberia, 2 vols. (New York,1960).

Jones, Adam, and Johnson, Marion, "Slaves from the Windward Coast," Journal of African History, 21 (1980), Vol. I, Pp.17-34.

Karnga, Abayomi. History of Liberia, publisher Liverpool, 1926

Moore, Bai T. "Liberian Culture at a Glance: a Review of the Culture and Customs of the Different Ethnic Groups in the Republic of Liberia," Monrovia, 1979.

Nelson, D.Harold. Liberia: A Country Study. (Foreign Area Studies, the American University. Sept. 1984). History of Liberia

Philip, Dray, At the Hands of Persons Unknown: the Lynching of Black America, Published in 2002.

"Parliament and the British Slave Trade 1600-1833." Retrieved on July 11, 2019, from www. Parliament.UK

Rodney, Walter, 'How Europe Underdeveloped Africa' (Dar-es-Salaam; London, 1973)

Slave Trade--Liberia, American State Papers 1st. Session 18th Congress, 12 Dec. 1822(Washington, D.C.,1822), P.1099 No.258.

"The African-American Mosaic - A Library of Congress Resource Guide for the study of Black History and Culture." Retrieved on July 10, 2019.

Wreh, Tuan, *The Love of Liberty: the rule of President William V.S. Tubman in Liberia, 1944-1971*, London; C. Hurst; New York; distributed by Universe Books, 1976.

___. (2017) "Liberia and the United States: A Complex Relationship." pbs.org. Global Connection. Retrieved on August 22, 2017.

William E. Allen, *Rethinking the History of Settler Agriculture in Nineteenth Century Liberia'(search/citation/490660),*" The International Journal of African Historical Studies Vol.37, No.3(2004):435-462

"*WEAH TAKES CHARGE,*" by Testimony Zeongar and Alfred Juteh Chea,(IMAGES), Liberian Societal, Lifestyle, Political Analysis, and Business Magazine,24th Edition/2017, Volume 2, Issue 18, Managing Editor Sando J. Moore

Walsh, Robert, *notice of Brazil in 1828 and 1829(1831). "Aboard a Slave Ship,1829,*" Eye witness to History; www.eyewithness to history.com Retrieved April17,2917

Zinn, Howard. *The People's History of the United States.* Publishers, 2005, 2009.